No Dinner For Sinners

A play

Edw

Samuel

www.sam

ISBN 978 0 573 11309 3

Please see page iv for further copyright information.

CHARACTERS

Jim Watt, businessman, 32
Helen Foster, Jim's girlfriend, 20s
Edna Chapman, Jim's cleaner, middle age
Terri Pringle, Jim's assistant, early 20s
Bill McGregor, Jim's boss, 50s
Nancy McGregor, Bill's wife, 40s

SYNOPSIS OF SCENES

The action of the play takes place in Jim Watt's apartment in Chelsea

ACT I
  SCENE 1 Saturday morning
  SCENE 2 Saturday afternoon

ACT II
  SCENE 1 Saturday evening
  SCENE 2 Ten minutes later

Time — the present

Other plays by Edward Taylor published by
Samuel French Ltd

Murder by Misadventure
Pardon Me, Prime Minister
Portrait of Fear
A Rise in the Market

ACT I
SCENE 1

The living-room of a smart, modern flat in Chelsea. Saturday morning

L *an arch leads into a small hall and the front door which can be seen.* US, *a passage leads to a kitchen, study and bathroom, which are probably unseen. Also* US *there is a long window, through which the sun is streaming in. There is a sofa, a well-stocked drinks cabinet and a coffee table. Part of the room is a dining area, where there is a dining table on which stands a vase of flowers.* R *two doors lead to bedrooms A and B. The door to bedroom A is open*

Electronic whoops and whizzes can be heard from the study, where someone is playing a loud computer pinball game. Normal computer noises are punctuated by occasional loud electronic raspberries. After a moment, the phone on the windowsill starts to ring

Helen (*off; calling from the bedroom*) Jim! Jim! The phone!

After a short while, Helen emerges from bedroom A, looking sleepy and wearing pyjamas and slippers. She's an attractive young woman in her twenties. She goes to the phone and picks up the receiver

Hello? ... Oh, hi Sophie. ... Well yes, I was, but don't worry. I had to get up anyway. The phone was ringing. ... No, Jim's in the study with the computer. First thing every day he has to check world share prices on the Internet. As you can hear, he's working hard. (*She holds the receiver up in the direction of the pinball noises for a moment; into the phone*) Well yes, it does sound rather like a computer pinball game, doesn't it? I expect he'll say it's market research. ... Oh thanks, but I got that news yesterday. Maxie left a message on my mobile. ... Yes, I'll be there at eleven. ... Oh, just the usual gear, I think. Should be fun. ... OK Sophie, thanks for calling. See you later.

Helen hangs up. The computer noise stops. Helen yawns, stretches, and heads for the kitchen

(*Muttering to herself*) Tea, tea, give me tea ...

She's intercepted by Jim, coming from the study. He's in his thirties and is wearing a towelling robe over his pyjamas

Jim Oh, hello darling. You're up.

Helen (*after a quick look at herself*) That's right, I am.

Jim Did I hear the phone?

Helen Evidently not, or you'd have answered it for us, wouldn't you?

Jim Ah. Well, I didn't think I'd get there in time.

Helen Poor old soul, it must be awful, having those arthritic legs.

Jim Sorry you didn't get your cup of tea in bed.

Helen Never mind, it might happen one day. Christmas perhaps?

Jim Oh, sooner than that.

Helen Whoopee. I'll go and put the kettle on.

Helen disappears into the kitchen

Jim stretches, then takes off his robe. He gets down on the floor and starts doing press-ups

After a moment, Helen enters from the kitchen, carrying a breakfast tray containing two glasses of water, Wheatipuffs, toast, milk, breadboard, cutlery, napkins, etc. She puts the tray on the dining table then looks quizzically at Jim's press-ups. She peers at the space underneath him

You're wasting your time, chum, the lady's not there any more.

Jim Oh God! Jokes at ten in the morning!

Helen starts spreading breakfast things on the table. Jim eventually feels he's suffered enough. He rises, staggers to the table and sits down, breathing heavily

Helen Are you sure that stuff is good for you?

Jim It must be, it's so painful. Lovely when you stop, though.

Helen How were the share prices?

Jim Oh, pretty stable. Rather dull, in fact.

Helen I suppose that's why you switched to pinball.

Jim Oh, you heard.

Helen And so did all the neighbours, I'm sure. Did you have fun?

Jim That wasn't fun, it was market research. Yakohito have brought out this new interactive super-game that blows raspberries when you miss. I thought I'd better check it out.

Helen You're so conscientious, Jim.

Jim Well, they could grab the whole market. Their shares are on the move already.

Helen I thought the markets were closed on Saturday.

Jim The London Stock Exchange is. But there's always an unofficial market. Brokers sitting up in bed, buying and selling on their laptops.

Helen Eugh. Please don't start doing that.

Jim I shan't while there are better things to do there.

Helen Thank God for that!

Jim And, of course, lots of markets all over the world do work at weekends. (*He consults his watch*) The Korean Stock Exchange opens in twenty minutes.

Helen The suspense is unbearable. I'll make the tea.

Jim Thanks.

Helen exits to the kitchen

Jim picks up a cereal packet and pours some cereal into his bowl. His attention is caught by the writing on the packet. He reads the back of it with interest, and then peers down inside the packet. Finally, he puts his hand in and gropes about. Having failed to find what he wanted, he crosses to the rear passage

(*Calling*) Helen!

Helen (*off; calling*) Yes?

Jim (*calling*) Are you having the Wheatipuffs?

Helen (*off; calling*) Probably.

Jim (*calling*) Oh, good.

Jim returns to the table, and empties the entire contents of the cereal packet on to the breadboard. He rummages about in the pile, and at last finds what he's looking for. He extracts a small object from the heap and dips it briefly into one of the glasses of water

Helen comes from the kitchen with two mugs of tea, and is appalled at the pile of cereal

Helen My God! What's happened to the Wheatipuffs? Did someone drop a bomb, or something?

Jim I tipped them out for you.

Helen The whole packet?

Jim (*picking up the packet and peering into it*) No, there's a couple still in there.

Helen You cretin! I can't eat that much! And I don't want them off the breadboard! (*Noticing some Wheatipuffs on the floor*) Or off the floor! Are you crazy?

Jim Sorry. I'll put them back.

Jim shoves handfuls of cereal back in the packet

Helen No! Not with your hand, stupid! You hold the packet open, I'll tip the breadboard.

They do so, and some Wheatipuffs fall on the table and the floor. Helen tidies up briefly and sits down

Dear God! It's like sharing a flat with a chimpanzee! What a mess! What the hell did you do that for?

Jim For the water pistol.

Helen Water pistol?

Jim There's a free miniature water pistol in every packet.

Helen You big baby! You're supposed to be running the London end of a big international firm!

Jim That doesn't mean I can't have fun!

Helen Fun? Playing with a kid's water pistol? You great fool! What's the point of it?

Jim It squirts water at people.

He squirts a small jet of water in her face

Helen Aagh! For God's sake! Did I say chimpanzee? It's like living with a retarded gibbon! (*She dabs her face with her napkin*)

Jim Go on. You love it, really.

Helen Like I loved Asian flu. Agh! It's made my jacket wet. You are an idiot!

Helen removes her pyjama jacket and starts dabbing her chest. Jim admires the view

Jim Hmm. I don't think that was so foolish actually. Let me help.

Jim advances his hand, with his napkin. Helen hits his hand sharply with a spoon

Helen That'll do. There's no time for any of that. I've got to be at Maxie's at eleven.

Jim Pity. Anyway, a drop of water never hurt anyone. Unless taken internally, of course. What's happening at Maxie's today?

Helen A photo shoot. Jewellery. (*She finishes drying her chest, then stands up*) I think I need a robe.

During the following, Helen goes to the bedroom, dons a robe from behind the door, and returns to the table

Jim You haven't forgotten the McGregors are coming to dinner?

Helen No, I haven't. Probably because you've reminded me every day this week. I've arranged to leave at four thirty, so I should be home by five.

Jim Good.

Helen Not good. The client's taking the girls out this evening. I've given up dinner at the *Savoy*, so I can entertain your friends!

Jim Thanks, darling. But they're not exactly friends, I just met him once, in New York. Basically this is business.

Helen All right, I'm staying home so I can help you suck up to the big boss. He is the big boss, right?

Jim They don't come much bigger. Bill McGregor is Wilson Keppel's International Director. Our London office is part of his empire.

Helen The jewel in his crown.

Jim Possibly. Anyway, he's doing his annual European tour.

Helen Oh yes, the European tour. "If it's Saturday, this must be London."

Jim He's a bit more thorough than that. He had two days in Rome last week, and managed to alter the computer system, change the investment policy, and bribe the trade minister. And he still had time to make twenty staff redundant.

Helen Ah. Sounds like a tough customer.

Jim As tough as an ingrown toenail, apparently. I'm relying on your elegant charm to melt his heart.

Helen I'll do my best. Just try to avoid squirting him with your water pistol. More tea?

Jim Yes, please.

Helen exits with the cups. Jim pours himself some cereal, and continues to study the packet while eating

The phone rings. Jim goes and picks up the receiver

Jim Watt. ... (*Surprised*) Oh, hello Terri. ... You're in the office today? ... Well, that's brilliant. ... Yes, of course, it would be great to have them done as soon as possible. ... Yes, I'll be here if you'd like to bring them over. But why don't you just fax them through? ... Oh, you need my signature. ... OK, any time. See you later. (*He hangs up and returns to his chair*)

Helen returns with more tea, and the two of them tackle their breakfast

Helen Who was that?

Jim Girl at the office. Terri Pringle. She's gone in today 'specially to finish some reports for me. She's bringing them round later.

Helen Well, well. Sounds like a fan of yours.

Jim She's a good kid. One of Wilson Keppel's brighter prospects. She's helpful to everyone.

Helen And pretty, I suppose?

Jim Er, yes, some of the blokes think so.

Helen Why am I beginning to dislike her?

Jim Perhaps you got out of bed the wrong side. She's a sweetie, honestly.

Helen That's what I'm afraid of.

Jim You needn't be, darling. I'm sure she can't cook like you. What are you giving the guests tonight?

Helen Tournedos chasseur.

Jim Pardon?

Helen Tournedos chasseur. I found a super recipe in *Marie Claire*.

Jim What is it?

Helen Best fillet steak on crispy croutes of fried bread, with a shallot and mushroom sauce, served with French beans à la Provencale — which means, with tomatoes, tiny onions, herbs and garlic.

Jim Ah. That should keep the vampires away.

Helen Oh, and pommes purées.

Jim (*a little dubious*) Yes. Are you sure you need all that elaborate stuff, darling? Couldn't you just roast a joint, or something?

Helen Of course not. Top people expect sophisticated dishes. Why do you ask?

Jim Oh, I just think these complicated things can make problems.

Helen Like what?

Jim Well, remember when you did sole veronique for the Becks? You let the brandy flame so high, your hair caught fire.

Helen It was only singed.

Jim Yes, but when Mrs Beck ran in to help, she slipped on the grape skins and sprained her ankle.

Helen Guests should stay out of the kitchen.

Jim Nevertheless, next day the Beck account went to Benson's.

Helen Well, at least that spared us having to tour their pig farm. Anyway, I'm doing tournedos chasseur. I've already got the ingredients. It's best if you leave these things to me.

Jim Ah. I'm sure it'll be delicious. Have you fixed for Edna to come and clean the flat this afternoon?

Helen Yes. Two 'til five. I've asked her to blitz the place. And, in particular, to get your chewing gum off the furniture. Right?

Jim OK. As long as she doesn't throw it away. Some of it may still be chewable.

Helen Eugh!

Jim She doesn't mind coming in on Saturday afternoon?

Helen No. She says it gets her away from her old man's TV football. And you're paying her double time, of course.

Jim Of course. As long as it helps towards a successful evening. Quite a lot depends on this, you know. Wilson Keppel are very fussy about their staff. I need to make a good impression.

Helen How could you fail, darling? As long as he sees you through Terri Pringle's eyes.

Jim (*tentatively*) Er ... There's one thing I have to ask you, Helen.

Helen Yes?

Jim Yes. Um, er, well ... We ought to be married.

Helen gasps

Helen (*after a moment's thought; ecstatic*) Jim! You mean it? I've waited two years for this! Darling, yes! We can get done at Chelsea Registry Office. I'll wear the white suit with the ——

Jim No, no, darling, I didn't mean actually married. I mean, we just have to tell the McGregors we are married.

Helen What?

Jim You see, he's an old-fashioned puritan. In fact, he's the President of Moral Outrage!

Helen What?

Jim You know, the anti-permissive society group. Since he took over at Wilson Keppel, he's enforced a strict moral code. Modesty boards on girls' desks. (*He laughs weakly*) We've even had to lose our *Playboy* calendars!

Helen is ominously silent, and glaring at Jim

So obviously he's very narrow-minded about sex. Moral Outrage is utterly opposed to unmarried couples living together. Even members of the opposite sex. So, as it's rather vital for my career, I thought you wouldn't mind if we gave him the impression that we're, well ... legal.

Helen (*flatly*) Legal.

Jim Yes. I mean, we probably won't have to actually lie. He'll assume we're married, we just needn't put him right. I mean, if he calls you Mrs Watt, don't deny it. Just say, "Please call me Helen."

Helen (*flatly*) Please call me Helen.

Jim That's right. Oh, and there's a sort of goldish ring among your costume jewellery. Perhaps you could stick that on your wedding finger.

Helen (*deadly calm*) Perhaps I could. But I think I have a better idea.

Jim Yes?

Helen I'll find that wide metal ring with the big knobbly stone on it.

Jim Big stone? That wouldn't look like a wedding ring.

Helen No. So I shan't stick it on my finger. I shall stick it right up your selfish, pompous backside!

Jim Helen!

Helen rises in fury and pounds the table with her fist. Jim wipes his eye, as milk splashes up from his cereal bowl

Helen How dare you! How *dare* you! You lying, arrogant, hypocritical toad!

Jim Helen, you're upset.

Helen You bet your life I'm upset! For two years I've shared your bed!

Jim Not all the time, we did get out occasionally.

Helen Two years we've been together, and I've put up with *Match of the Day* and falling over golf clubs! Not to mention your puerile jokes! Two years, and you've never once mentioned marriage!

Jim I thought you liked your independence.

Helen You never asked, did you? And now, the first time you say the word, it's a mockery. I'm expected to con this American freak, just to save your rotten skin!

Jim Helen, listen ——

Helen No, you listen! The answer is no! Absolutely categorically, and finally no! (*She strides off towards bedroom A*) I'm getting out of here! It stinks of hypocrisy!

The following dialogue is shouted as Helen goes into bedroom A and does a quick change with the door open

Jim, agitated, hovers outside

Jim Helen, you haven't finished your breakfast.

Helen (*off*) No, and I haven't had my shower either. I'll do all that at Maxie's.

Jim I'm sorry if I said the wrong thing.

Helen (*off*) No, you said the right thing. You finally let me know where I stand. I'm just a convenience! A temporary trollop! Not to be taken seriously! Wife for a night, and then back to bimbo! A one-night-stand spread over two years!

Jim Helen, please ——

Helen (*off*) Will you shut up and let me get a word in? And don't come in here, stay outside!

Jim All right, darling, but listen. If I hadn't warned you about Bill McGregor's ideas, tonight could have got a bit awkward. I just wanted to smooth things over.

Helen (*off*) You're so damn smooth, it's a wonder your trousers stay up! Not that they do, half the time!

Jim You know what I mean. I don't want you embarrassed this evening.

Helen (*off*) Don't worry, I shan't be embarrassed, because I won't be here!

Jim What?

Helen (*off*) I was giving up a night out, wasn't I, so I could cook for you and your cronies. But not any more. If anyone wants me, I'll be at the Savoy. Under my own name. Mzzz Foster.

Jim Helen, you can't do this! Who's going to cook our dinner?

Helen (*off*) You don't trust my cooking, you can have a go yourself! The food's in the fridge, the recipe's in *Marie Claire*, on the kitchen shelf.

Jim But I need a hostess, a wife.

Helen (*off*) Try the twenty-four-hour Marriage Bureau. Only don't tell them what a smug, conniving bastard you are, or they'll pair you off with Lucrezia Borgia!

Helen now emerges from bedroom A in day clothes. She's carrying a small holdall and making for the front door

I'm moving out, Jim. I'll send someone over for my things tomorrow.

Jim Helen, I'd no idea you felt so strongly.

Helen Well, you know now. Goodbye, Jim — and don't think it hasn't been fun, because it hasn't!

Jim is desperate. He grabs Helen's arm

Jim Helen, for heaven's sake! Let's sit down and discuss this.

Helen Let go of me!

Jim Please, darling! Give me a moment!

Helen There's only one thing I want to give you, Jim Watt ...

Helen shakes her arm free. The vase of flowers is close at hand. Swiftly, she plucks out the flowers and empties the water from the vase over Jim's head

Jim Aaagh!
Helen Remember, a drop of water never hurt anyone! Unless taken internally!

The Lights fade to Black-out

SCENE 2

The same. It is 4 p.m. that afternoon

Edna Chapman is hoovering Jim's lounge with a very noisy hoover. She's a short, chunky lady in her fifties, wearing a pink overall and she has a cigarette end drooping from the corner of her mouth

As she approaches the area where the breakfast table stood, she notices the Wheatipuffs on the floor and is intrigued. She switches off the hoover, picks up a Wheatipuff, wipes it on her overall, and pops it in her mouth. She likes it, so she picks up some more and puts them in her overall pocket

As she's about to resume hoovering, the phone rings. She lifts the receiver, and puts on a posh voice

Edna (*into the phone*) Mr Watt's residence. ... Yes, I think he's available. Who shall I say is calling? ... One moment, please.

Edna lays the receiver beside the phone, moves towards the study, and shouts in her normal, raucous cockney voice

  Oi! Mr Watt! Some woman called Stephanie on the blower!

Edna resumes hoovering

  Jim emerges from the study, carrying a pen and notebook

Jim (*shouting over the hoover*) Thank you, Edna. (*Into the phone; loudly*) Hello? ... Hello? ... Stephanie? ... (*To Edna*) I'm sorry, Edna, I can't hear with that thing on.

Edna Pardon?

Jim (*shouting and gesturing*) I can't hear with that thing on! Switch it off, please, Edna! *Off!*

Edna switches the hoover off

Edna Sorry, Mr Watt, couldn't hear you for the hoover.

Jim Yes. Could you do something quiet for a bit, like dusting?

Edna Do you mind? I've already dusted in here!

Jim Well, perhaps some more dust will have settled by now.

Edna (*sniffing*) Well, I'll do a bit of polishing.

Edna goes to the kitchen. During the following, she returns with a duster and a polish spray, with which she attacks various surfaces

Jim (*into the phone*) Sorry, Stephanie, thanks for ringing back. It's been a long time. Any chance of joining me for dinner tonight? I thought it was time we got together again. … (*Disappointed*) Oh. Oh, I see. … Oh, your husband, yes. … And your child, really? … Children, sorry. Gosh, it has been a long time. … No, I just wanted to see you again, that's all. … (*Unenthusiastically*) Lunch some time, yes, why not? I'll give you a ring when things are quieter. … Sorry, I'll have to go now, I have a visitor. *Ciao*, Stephanie. (*He hangs up*) Blast!

He opens his notebook and crosses out a name on a list. He sighs, and we sense that a lot of names have been crossed off already. He reads another name from the notebook, and dials a number

Hello. Is Jane Fletcher there, please? … Oh, is that you Jane? This is rather a bad line, I can't hear you very well. … Ah, that's better. It's Jim Watt. … Jim Watt! You remember, sexy Jim! You haven't forgotten those passionate weekends when your parents were away? Have you still got that dimple on your —— Pardon? … You're her mother. Oh my God. Ah, sorry to trouble you, Mrs Fletcher. … Yes, I wanted a word with Jane. … Gone to Australia? Ah, I'm not surprised. … You didn't catch what? … Oh, my name's Tony Blair. Give her my love. Goodbye.

He replaces the receiver, and crosses another name off his list

Number ten down the drain.

Edna You're in trouble, Mr Watt, aren't you?

Jim I certainly am, Edna. I've got my boss coming to dinner tonight, and I promised he'd meet my wife.

Edna You haven't got a wife.

Jim No, but I was hoping Miss Foster might do the job for tonight.

Edna And she won't?

Jim No, she's walked — I mean she has to work this evening.

Edna Go on. She's walked out on you, hasn't she?

Jim How did you guess?

Edna Oh, little things. Her toothbrush gone from the bathroom, the overturned chair in the bedroom ...

Jim Well, you're right, of course. She stormed out at breakfast-time.

Edna Something upset her, did it?

Jim You could say that.

Edna Never mind, she'll be back.

Jim I doubt it. Anyway, she certainly won't be here this evening.

Edna Shame. Still, it's not the end of the world, is it?

Jim It might be the end of my job. If I don't produce a wife to meet my boss, I'm in big trouble. He thinks bachelors get up to mischief.

Edna Well, they do if you pick the right ones.

Jim And if he heard I was living with a partner, he'd explode!

Edna (*incredulously*) You're joking! Everyone lives with partners these days. Most people think nothing of it.

Jim Mr McGregor isn't "most people". He's a fanatical puritan. His mother was bitten by a rabid monk!

Edna Oh. Religious, is he?

Jim Very. And he's president of a morality group. He insists all his managers must be family men, and go to church on Sunday. And apart from all that, I need someone to cook the meal.

Edna What about all them girlfriends you had before Miss Foster moved in?

Jim I've been trying them, Edna. That's what all the phone calls are about. (*He consults his list*) Four unobtainable, three married, two emigrated, one wouldn't help.

Edna Turned you down?

Jim In the end. She was happy to meet me for dinner. But when I told her it meant coming here and cooking it, she hung up for some reason.

Edna People are funny, aren't they? What about that nice girl with the red hair — Shirley, was it?

Jim Shirley Wilson, my last hope. She was out, but her flatmate said she'd get her to ring back. She lives just down the road, in Kensington.

Edna Oh, that's nice. Actress, isn't she?

Jim When she's working.

Edna She'd be all right, acting the part of your wife.

Jim Yes, I think she might relish the challenge.

Edna I liked Shirley. She always had a friendly word.

Jim Yes. Some of her words got a bit unfriendly towards the end, but I hope she'll let bygones be bygones. We certainly had some good times.

The phone rings. Jim picks up the receiver

Jim Watt here. ... (*Warmly*) Shirley, hello! Thanks for ringing back. How are you? ... (*At first it seems his warmth is reciprocated*) Oh good. Keeping busy, I hope? ... Ah well, a walk-on's better than nothing, isn't it? ... Anyway, long time no see. Too long, in fact. Did Karen tell you, I thought we might get together for a spot of dinner tonight. ... Yes. What do you think? ... (*He is shaken by the force of a non-stop diatribe*) Not for what? ... What? ... Go and boil my what? ... Shirley, please! ... Listen, I —— (*To Edna*) Oh, she's gone. (*He sadly replaces the receiver*)

Edna Any luck?

Jim In a way. She says she never wants to speak to me again. But that doesn't help for tonight.

Edna Well, who'd have thought she'd turn nasty like that?

Jim I'm not surprised, she always had a temper. A bit like a corked volcano. It's the red hair, you know.

Edna Anyone else you can try?

Jim I think there may be one more name, in my old Filofax. (*As he goes to the study*) I'm beginning to think it's not my day.

He exits

Edna continues her polishing activities. She points the polish spray at some smart piece of furniture and presses the top but nothing happens. She shakes the can furiously and tries again, once more with no result. She shakes and tries again several more times, and then gives up. The can is empty

Edna Oh well. (*She spits heartily into her duster and applies it vigorously to the surface*)

The doorbell rings. Edna goes and opens the front door

Terri Pringle, a pretty girl in her early twenties stands there. Terri wears glasses and carries a slim briefcase. It will become clear that she hero-worships Jim

Terri Hi. I've brought some papers for Mr Watt.

Edna Oh, that's nice. Is he expecting you?
Terri Yes, I'm Terri Pringle, from his office.
Edna Well, you'd better come in then.

Edna closes the front door, and precedes Terri into the living-room

As they enter, Jim returns from the study

Jim It's no use, I've just remembered. I threw that old Filofax away. Did I hear the doorbell?
Edna Yes. Miss Dingle's here from your office.
Jim What? Oh, Terri, hello. You're looking very smart, as usual. Thanks for coming over.
Terri That's all right, Mr Watt. I'm sorry to disturb you. But I need your signature on these reports before I fax them to the States.

She takes a sheaf of papers from her briefcase and puts them on the coffee table

Jim Well, that's easily done. Do make yourself at home. This is Mrs Chapman, who does for me.
Terri Pleased to meet you, Mrs Chapman.
Edna Likewise, I'm sure.
Jim Can I get you a drink, Terri?
Terri Well, it's a bit early for a tipple, isn't it? But I wouldn't say no to a fruit juice. Orange, if you've got it.
Jim Shall be done. Edna?
Edna No thanks, I'll make a nice pot of tea in a minute.

Jim exits to the kitchen

Edna continues polishing. Terri is looking around

Terri This is a lovely flat, isn't it?
Edna It is, unless you have to clean it. Too many nooks and crannies for my liking.
Terri Oh. Well, it's a nice view from the window.
Edna It would be, if it wasn't for them houses opposite. They're a real eyesore.
Terri Oh. Yes, it's a pity about the houses. Apart from them, it's a lovely view.
Edna Except for them big adverts. I hate them enormous posters, don't you? People with rows of teeth twenty-foot wide. Reminds me of Hoxton Cemetery.

Terri Yes. Yes, they are big, aren't they? Ahem. D'you come here every day, Mrs Chapman?

Edna No. Usually Monday and Thursday. But Mr Watt's having a do, so I made Monday a Wednesday this week, and Thursday Saturday. Of course, I could have made next week's Monday this Saturday and turned Thursday into Wednesday, but I thought this was easier.

Terri Yes. I'm sure you're right.

Edna Fridays, I do the Parker-Browns. (*Proudly*) They've got a big house in Cheyne Walk!

Terri Really?

Edna Oh yes. Very posh, they are. Grapes in the house when nobody's ill!

Jim returns with a glass of fruit juice, a can of beer and a glass

Jim Here we are, Terri. Do sit down.

Terri Thanks. (*She takes her glass and sits on the sofa*)

Jim I've finished in the study for a while, Edna, if you'd like to have a go in there.

Edna All right, as long as you've got your papers off the floor. I'm here as a cleaner, not a refuse collector.

Jim I've shoved all the loose stuff under the desk. There's a nice clear space in the middle of the floor that's ideal for hoovering.

Edna (*as she leaves*) OK, if you say so. But you'll have to let me get under that desk some time. There's enough dust down there to grow potatoes.

Edna exits

Jim pours out his beer into a glass and sits next to Terri. He looks at the sheaf of papers on the low table in front of him as Terri gets a pen

Jim Now then, I'll just sign these. (*He looks around*) Ah, I'll need a pen. (*Noticing the pen*) Thanks.

Terri You need to sign each page where I've put the little cross. I've pulled together all the investment figures for the month. That's what New York asked for.

Jim What would I do without you, Terri?

Terri Well, I always think top executives should be left free to think about the big decisions. Leave details to people like me.

Jim (*signing the papers*) I wish there were more people like you, young lady. (*He reads the papers; alarmed*) My God, did we really put five million into Cooler Telecom?

Terri Yes, but it's all right. We got out before they collapsed.

Jim We were lucky.

Terri Well, it wasn't just luck. I saw a tip in the paper, so I told Mr Witherspoon and he sold at once.

Jim Terri, you're a treasure. (*Signing*) There, that's finished. "Something attempted, something done, has earned a night's repose," my mother used to say.

Terri Thank you, Mr Watt. I'd better leave you in peace. (*She gathers the papers and starts to rise*)

Jim No no, don't go yet. I'd like to talk to you.

Terri (*sitting down again*) Oh ... Well, thank you, Mr Watt. If you've got the time.

Jim I may have something to ask you later.

Terri Ooh! That sounds exciting.

Jim You're a worker, Terri, and you've got initiative. I think you could go a long way in this business. With the right help and support.

Terri I'm glad you think so, Mr Watt. But I'm not sure I really want to.

Jim No? You've always struck me as a career girl.

Terri Yes, but not in finance.

Jim No? What's your big ambition then?

Terri I want to be an actress.

Jim Really? That's interesting. But you didn't go to drama school?

Terri No, well, I've got to earn a living, haven't I? I'm doing drama in my spare time.

Jim Very enterprising.

Terri I've joined the Parthenon Theatre Company. They're one of the best theatre groups in London.

Jim The Parthenon. Where are they based?

Terri In Hornsey. Near my flat. They're very good, because they put on really worthwhile plays. Not thrillers and comedies and all that stuff. They do challenging things. New plays. Drama that confronts important issues.

Jim Are you doing something at the moment?

Terri Yes, it's a real masterpiece. A new play by Kurt Grimm, called *The Naked Dance*.

Jim *The Naked Dance.*

Terri The title's symbolic, of course. There's no actual dancing.

Jim I see.

Terri Grimm sees life as a ritual dance. Everyone thinks they're doing their own thing, but really they're following a routine. And, however we try to cover ourselves, anyone can see what we really are.

Jim That's an alarming thought.

Terri Yes, but it's valid, isn't it? And I've got a smashing part — lots of nice showy bits. I go mad in act two, and attack my mum with a bicycle pump.

Jim A bicycle pump?

Terri Yes. It was supposed to be a Geiger counter, but we couldn't get hold of one. It's a phallic symbol, of course.

Jim Of course. Well, well. All that excitement in your life, and you're still prepared to come to work on a Saturday.

Terri Well, today was special, Mr Watt. It was for your sake. You might have been in trouble if we hadn't got this lot off today.

Jim Thank you, Terri. I'm touched.

Terri And, actually, I wouldn't *mind* being promoted in Wilson Keppel. In case I don't make it as an actress. I enjoy both really, I like meeting people.

Jim D'you find it a good atmosphere in our office?

Terri Oh yes. And that's thanks to you. Everyone's really, well, you know … motivated.

Jim I'm glad to hear it.

Terri I do admire you, Mr Watt. You're so clever, so decisive.

Jim (*disputing*) Oh, come along, Terri …

Terri No no, it's true, you are.

Jim I wasn't arguing. I was just going to say, please call me Jim.

Terri Oh, can I really? Thank you, Mr Watt.

Jim Is your boyfriend keen on the theatre?

Terri I haven't got a boyfriend at the moment. Well, not a serious one.

Jim I'm surprised.

Terri Well, I'm a bit choosy, to be honest. I fancied Jason, our director at the drama group. He's a great looking bloke. But it turned out we have too much in common.

Jim Too much in common?

Terri Yes. We're both keen on boys.

Jim Oh, I see.

Terri Last year I was going out with Nick Newman, in Research. But he's obsessed with computers. He spends so much time getting virtual sex on the Internet, he's forgotten what to do with real girls.

Jim Shame. I don't know what's happened to the younger generation.

Terri The boys are short of hormones, aren't they? 'Cause of all the chemicals they put in the water these days.

Jim Ah, is that it?

Terri Tell the truth, I prefer older men. I don't mean really ancient, like forty. Just sort of early thirties. That's you, isn't it, Mr Watt?

Jim I'm thirty-two. It's the oldest I've ever been.

Terri I think that's the perfect age for a chap.

Jim Good. I must say, I quite like it. Tell me, Terri, d'you have any
hobbies? Cooking, for instance?

Terri Oh yes, I love cooking. When I go home to Mum and Dad's, I
always cook Sunday lunch.

Jim That's nice for them.

Terri Well, they're a bit conservative. Last month I did them lasagne
verde al forno and they said, why couldn't they have rissoles?

Jim (*thoughtfully*) Lasagne verde al forno sounds wonderful. (*He has
clearly made a decision*) I must say, Terri, you should do well as an
actress. You've got the necessary good looks.

Terri Oh, go on! D'you really think so?

Jim Undoubtedly. The shape of the head, the classic features. D'you
have to wear those glasses all the time?

Terri No, I don't *have* to …

Jim Good. (*He leans forward and removes Terri's glasses*) With glasses,
my dear, you're very pretty. Without them, you're beautiful.

Jim kisses Terri's hand. She reacts with enthusiasm

Terri Hang on a minute, I'll put this down.

*She goes to put her drink down on the table, misses, and drops her half
full glass on Jim's foot*

Oh dear, sorry! You see, I don't *have* to wear glasses, but it's best if I
do, because without them I can't see.

*Jim returns Terri's glasses. She puts them on while he dries his shoe and
sock with a handkerchief. He then puts her drinking glass back on the
table*

Jim Never mind, the carpet's pretty ancient.

Terri But your foot's all wet, you'll get rheumatism.

Jim I'll survive. Have you tried contact lenses?

Terri I can't wear them. They make my eyes water, and I'm always
losing them. I've swallowed at least two.

Jim Pity. Perhaps if we got you the new expensive ones, they might
work better. Anyway, glasses or no glasses, you're a very attractive
girl, as I said.

Terri I wish I thought so.

Jim There's no doubt about it. I'm amazed the boys aren't all round
you, like bees round a honeypot.

Terri Well, thank you, Mr Watt. I'm sure you know about these things.

Jim takes her hands and draws her closer to him. As their lips meet, the hoover is switched on

Edna bursts in, pushing the hoover in front of her

Edna All right to carry on now, is it then?

Jim and Terri spring apart

Jim Not really, Edna. Miss Pringle and I still have some business to sort out.
Edna (*taking in the scene*) Oh. So I see. Oh well, I'll do the bedrooms then.

Edna directs the hoover in a sharp right turn, and disappears into bedroom A, closing the door behind her

Jim Sorry about that, Terri. I was taking rather a lot for granted.
Terri That's all right, Mr Watt, you go ahead. I like a fast worker.
Jim Ah. I'm afraid the moment's passed. I think a hoover must be one of the world's great passion killers.
Terri Some other time then?
Jim Yes, please. The fact is, Terri, I've got something on my mind ... A problem you might be able to help me with.
Terri You know I'd do anything for you, Mr Watt.
Jim Careful. You'd better find out what it is first.
Terri Yes?
Jim One of the big bosses is over from America, and he and his wife are coming here to dinner. He's very strong on traditional morality, expects all his managers to be family men.
Terri Oh yes, I heard something about that.
Jim I've promised he'll meet my wife. And I haven't got one.
Terri But you've got a partner, haven't you? That's what they say in the office. You can just pretend you're married.
Jim That's what I was planning to do. But Helen's wal — I mean, she has to be away. So I've got no wife, no hostess, and no one to cook the dinner. I wondered if you'd like to take on the job for the night.
Terri (*joyous*) Ooh, Mr Watt!
Jim Your chance for a bit of cooking, and acting as well.
Terri Mr Watt, I'd love to! I could do beef wellington. Americans love that. When are they coming?
Jim Helen went off at rather short notice, I'm afraid. I'm talking about tonight.

Terri (*hugely disappoined*) Oh no! Oh, sod it! I've got a rehearsal tonight, Mr Watt, and I can't get out of it! *The Naked Dance* opens in ten days.

Jim Oh dear. Ah well … You didn't mind my asking?

Terri Not at all. Any other time I'd love to be your wife, in any way you like.

Jim Well, thank you, Terri. That's good to know. And thanks for the reports.

Terri (*picking up the papers*) I'll get back to the office, and fax these to the States before midday their time. (*She gets up*) I'm ever so sorry I can't help you tonight, Mr Watt. *The Naked Dance* is my big chance.

Jim I quite understand, Terri. And would you please have another shot at calling me Jim? Mr Watt makes me feel about eighty!

Terri I'm sorry, Mr Wa— Jim. I suppose it's 'cause of you being in charge.

Jim Well, that may not be a problem much longer, if I can't find a wife for tonight. Never mind, I'd better let you go now, Terri. I've got some thinking to do.

Terri Right-o, Jim. I'll let myself out.

Jim No no, let me come and open the door.

Jim and Terri go to the hall

Terri exits through the front door

The door of bedroom A opens and Edna enters with the hoover roaring. She's reached the space behind the sofa when she sees Jim and switches the hoover off

Edna Nice young lady. I think she fancies you.

Jim She might not, when I'm out of a job.

Edna Well, why don't you ask her to be your wife for tonight?

Jim I did. She would have done, but she can't. She's not free. (*He consults his watch*) My God! The McGregors arrive in three hours! They'll find me all on my own with a heap of raw food, like a mangy lion with no teeth.

Edna Listen, why don't you just cancel? Ring these people and call it off? Say your wife's ill.

Jim I thought of that, but I've forgotten which hotel they're in.

Edna Didn't you make a note?

Jim Yes, but I've forgotten where I put it.

Edna Ring round all the big hotels.

Jim By the time I hit the right one, they could have started out. Besides, I don't really want to cancel. I've got some ideas to put to McGregor that could do me a lot of good.

Edna Tell him another time then.

Jim He goes back to the States next week. This is my only chance. (*He sighs*) I can't believe all those girls turned me down.

Edna Fair-weather friends, I call them.

Jim There must be some woman somewhere who'd help me out.

Edna There is. But you keep looking in the wrong direction.

Jim Wrong direction?

Edna All them young, good time girlfriends of yours. They won't put themselves out when you're in trouble. You need a mature woman, who'll stand by a man. Someone who's cleaned for you and looked after you for years.

Jim Edna, I can't ask my mother to pose as my wife! That's tantamount to incest! Besides, she's in Torquay.

Edna Not your mother, Mr Watt!

Jim I don't know any other mature women.

Edna Yes, you do. Just look straight ahead. (*She strikes a coquettish pose*)

Jim (*truth dawning*) Edna! You mean ...

Edna Of course, I ought to feel offended you never asked me in the first place. I suppose you don't think I'm good enough.

Jim (*desperately evasive*) Not at all, Edna, certainly not — my word, no! But — but ... I mean, you're a married woman. What would Mr Chapman say?

Edna He'd never even notice. Saturday nights, he's down the pub with his mates. By the time he gets home, he's so pie-eyed, he has trouble finding his way upstairs!

Jim He might ask questions tomorrow.

Edna Then I'll tell him the truth. There'll be nothing to hide, will there? Worse luck! I'm only offering to cook for you and chat up your guests, aren't I?

Jim Yes, but ...

Edna I used to do quite a few catering jobs, before my feet got too bad. So what about it?

Jim (*still desperately evasive*) It's very kind of you, Edna, but really, I mean ...

Edna You *don't* think I'm good enough, do you? Not the right class.

Jim Good grief, it's nothing to do with class! All that went out of the window years ago!

Edna Not in Battersea it didn't.

Jim Well, it did here. Of course you're good enough, Edna. It's just that, well, the McGregors are high-powered business people. You wouldn't have much to talk about.

Edna Oh, I can always find lots to talk about. "Chatty Chapman" they call me down our street.

Jim I'm not sure you'd enjoy it, Edna.

Edna I'm not expecting to enjoy it, am I? We're talking about a professional job.

Jim Ah. You're thinking of a fee.

Edna I've thought of one. Thirty quid I used to get for catering, five years ago. That's worth fifty now. Then there's the same for chatting. Call it a hundred, and I'll give them my hotpot.

Jim Well, the fee's no problem. But you see, Edna … How can I put this? I mean, will we look convincing as husband and wife?

Edna Why not? We can have a row in the kitchen, just like anyone else!

Jim Yes, but … I don't want to seem unchivalrous, but, well, what about the age difference?

Edna Gawd, they'll never notice that! You haven't seen me with my hair done and my make-up on. They'll think you married Madonna!

Jim If you say so, but honestly …

The phone rings. Jim picks up the receiver

Jim Watt. … Oh, hello, Pierre. … Yes, they're coming here this evening. … Ah, I heard they'd been in Paris, yes. … He did what? You can't do that sort of thing these days! … Oh, in France you can? … Ah, I see. (*Shaken*) My God! That would be the same here, wouldn't it? Poor old Louis. Well, thanks for the tip-off, Pierre. … Yes, I'll let you know what happens. *Au revoir*. (*He hangs up; despondently*) Bill McGregor fired a senior man in Paris, because he was living with his girlfriend.

Edna Gordon Bennett! He's a monster! But they can't just go and sack people like that. Can they?

Jim McGregor told him he'd be transferred to our office in Afghanistan. So Louis resigned.

Edna That's wicked! Well, Mr Watt, you are in trouble!

Jim All right, Edna. You said a hundred, right?

Edna A hundred quid, that's right.

Jim I'll make it a hundred and fifty, if you can bring it off!

Edna I'll do that all right, don't you worry. Of course, I'll need to get my hair done, that'll be extra.

Jim All right, but you'll have to be quick.

Edna Let's hope Emilio's still open.

Jim There's a ladies' salon just opposite.

Edna If you want Madonna, it's got to be Emilio. And I'll need to nip home for a frock.

Jim Take a taxi.

Edna I was going to. But there's still not much time to get stuff for the hotpot. You'll have to do the shopping. I'll give you a list.

Jim Don't worry about that, Miss Foster got lots of food in. She was going to do some recipe from her magazine — tournedos chasseur, I think she said, with French beans and funny mushrooms.

Edna Oh yeah, I think I've heard of that.

Jim On the other hand, it might be easier if you just grilled the steak and fried the mushrooms. Keep it simple.

Edna No, if Miss Foster was going to do tornadoes chassis, so can I. Make it like one of them posh nosh meals on telly. I expect she left the recipe out.

Jim On the kitchen shelf, she said.

Edna Well, that's it then. I'll nip home, get the barnet done, pick up a dress, and be back by six. It'll be a great evening.

Jim I hope so.

Edna Shall I get a bottle of plonk, to make the party go with a swing?

Jim No thanks, Edna. I've got all the booze we need.

Edna That's if he drinks, of course. You said he's religious, so he might not.

Jim Don't worry, there's plenty of Coca-Cola. All Americans drink Coca-Cola, it's compulsory.

Edna Right, well, I'll be off then. Oh, and Mr Watt.

Jim Yes?

Edna All these interruptions, I haven't finished the cleaning. You'll have to do it.

Jim Me?

Edna There's no one else, is there? I haven't done the main bathroom or the small bedroom. And I haven't finished in here. So you'll have to get down to it.

Jim Is that necessary? The place looks OK.

Edna It does not. I'm not entertaining our friends in a pigsty! You'd better start by hoovering over there. (*She points to the area behind the sofa, where she's left the hoover*) And there's not much time, so you'll need to get on with it!

Jim Oh well, if you say so. (*He trudges over to behind the sofa*)

Edna I do. And don't forget, you'll need a bath before the guests come. Watch out for that lead!

Jim Pardon? ... Aaagh!

Jim trips over the hoover lead and falls with a cry

Edna Oh my gawd, I warned you!

A moment later Jim's head appears above the back of the sofa

Oh well, you're not hurt. So you can get started. If we're going to be
married, you'll have to learn to do as you're told!

Jim groans

The Lights fade to Black-out

ACT II
Scene 1

The same. It is 7.20 p.m. that evening

It is dark outside and pleasantly lit within. Jim is wearing a grey suit and a red tie and is laying the table for dinner. The task is almost completed, though not very expertly. He puzzles over some cutlery in his hand. He puts a spoon down to the left of a place mat, but decides it doesn't look right, so he moves it to the right, but it still looks wrong. He tries laying it across the top, but is again dissatisfied. He picks up the spoon and looks at it

Jim (*calling toward bedroom A*) Edna!

Edna (*off; calling from bedroom A*) Hang on, Mr Watt, I'm just finishing my eyebrows. I'll be with you in a minute.

Jim We haven't much time! It's twenty past seven!

Edna (*off*) All right. I know that, I'm coming!

Jim I have a problem.

Edna (*off*) OK, I'm here.

Now glamourized for the evening, Edna appears in the bedroom A doorway and strikes a pose. She is wearing a rather appalling dress and has an exotic hairstyle

There! How do I look?

Jim Er ... Remarkable. A transformation. Not a lot like Madonna.

Edna Emilio says she's past it. This is an original creation. Emilio says there's nothing else like it!

Jim That I can believe. Edna, what are these little spoons for?

Edna Melon.

Jim Melon?

Edna I found one in the fridge, so I'm using it for starters.

Jim Well done, good idea. Where do the spoons go?

Edna Right-hand side of the mat. And them titchy little forks go opposite, on the left.

Jim Ah, right. (*He puts the cutlery in place*)

Edna I couldn't find cherries for the melon slices. So I've given each of them a dollop of strawberry jam.

Jim Sounds delicious. Have you started the main course yet?

Edna No, but don't worry, I found the recipe and got the stuff out. The first job is chopping all them veggies for the sauce. (*Noticing flaws in the table setting*) Haven't you done that table yet?

Jim Yes, I've just finished.

Edna No, you haven't, there's no tablespoons. You have to serve at the table for these posh do's, you know. You can't just dish it all out in the kitchen like at home.

Jim (*as he goes*) All right, I think I know where to find tablespoons.

Jim exits to the kitchen

Edna (*calling*) And bring the salt and pepper while you're at it!

Jim (*off; calling*) Salt and pepper, right.

Edna surveys the table, in proprietorial fashion. She straightens some mats and cutlery then puts her fingers underneath to move the table slightly

Edna Eugh! There's something nasty under the table!

Jim enters

Jim Something nasty? Don't say the next door cat's been in again!

Edna No! Sticking to the bottom of the table! Yuk! It's chewing gum!

Jim Oh, ah … Chewing gum, yes. I've asked Miss Foster not to leave it around, but she can't seem to give it up. I'll take it.

Jim puts the spoons and a cruet on the table. He takes the piece of chewing gum from underneath and puts it in his handkerchief, which he returns to his pocket

Edna Nasty habit. My nephew's always got chewing gum in. Drives his teachers mad.

Jim Oh well, it's better than smoking.

Edna He does that as well. But it's the chewing that gets up my nose. Chewing and sucking. (*Imitating the noise*) Like a cow pulling its foot out of the mud.

Jim It doesn't have to be like that, you know. You can chew quietly. (*He checks the drinks cabinet*)

Edna Shane just likes upsetting people. Still he's better than his brother, that I will say. Dean's been done again for nicking hubcaps.

Jim Oh dear. Perhaps it was a mistake.

Edna Don't you believe it! A fiver for ten hubcaps he gets down the scrapyard. Pays for his fags.

Jim Yes. Ahem. Er, there's no need to mention your family to the McGregors, Edna, is there? Just stick to general topics. The weather, and so on.

Edna Don't worry, Mr Watt. I won't let you down. I've got plenty of religious chat to give them.

Jim Religious chat?

Edna You said they're religious.

Jim Very. Well, he is, for sure.

Edna Yeah, well, I know all that stuff. My uncle was verger down the Reform Chapel. 'Til they caught him at the communion wine.

Jim I see.

Edna So I can do them lots of church talk. That'll please them.

Jim Well, yes, but don't overdo it.

Edna (*inspecting Jim*) That tie's not right with your suit, you know. Looks like your tongue's hanging out.

Jim Oh well, it's too late now, it'll have to do.

Edna That's not the right attitude, Mr Watt. If you want to impress these people, you need to show them you have good taste. Luckily, that's something I've always had.

Jim I'd better open some red wine, give it a chance to breathe. (*Taking a bottle from the cabinet and drawing the cork*) Is the table all right now?

Edna Yes, I think that's everything. Oh, gawd no! I know what we've forgot! We haven't put out any nibbles.

Jim Ah, you mean crisps and things. Sorry, we haven't got any, as far as I know.

Edna Nuts?

Jim No, we don't use them.

Edna You can't offer guests drinks without nibbles. If they've nothing to do with their hands, they knock back too much booze.

Jim Oh dear. That's the sort of thing Miss Foster might have thought of. It would never occur to me.

Edna Tell you what, I found some very tasty titbits on the floor here, when I was hoovering. I think they were Wheatipuffs. They look like nibbles.

Jim Ah. Yes. But I'm afraid I emptied the packet.

Edna (*moving off to the kitchen*) Never mind, I picked some up and put them in my pocket. My overall's in the kitchen. (*Remembering*) Oh, and I found a little rubber water pistol on the floor. I expect it came from the cereal packet. Shall I throw it away?

Jim What? (*Remembering*) Ah, the water pistol. No, that's mine, I might need it. Find somewhere safe to put it, would you? I'm having a drink. Shall I pour one for you, Edna?
Edna No thanks, I'll wait.

She exits

Jim pours himself a gin and tonic from the drinks cabinet

Edna returns from the kitchen carrying a small glass bowl of Wheatipuffs, which she puts down somewhere handy

There, at least that's something to offer them. I got all the fluff off.
Jim Yes, they look all right.
Edna I'd better shut myself in the kitchen and get on with the dinner.

She moves off towards the kitchen. Jim hands her a bottle of white wine from the cabinet

Jim Put the white wine in the fridge, will you?
Edna Right, Mr Watt.
Jim Oh, and Edna …
 Edna Yes?
Jim The guests might be a bit surprised to hear my wife calling me Mr Watt. Can you remember to say Jim?
Edna I'll try, Mr Watt. And don't drink too much of that stuff. If I drink this early, I'm squiffy by dinnertime!

Edna exits and we hear the kitchen door shut

Jim gulps down his drink and pours himself another

The doorbell rings. Jim straightens his tie, goes to the front door and opens it

The Americans are there. Bill McGregor is a tough, sturdy businessman in his fifties. His wife, Nancy, is smart and attractive, probably in her forties

Jim (*warmly*) Hello! Come in, Mr McGregor. Good to see you again! Mrs McGregor, welcome!
Bill Hi. The name's Bill. And this is my wife, Nancy.
Jim How do you do. I'm Jim Watt.

Nancy A pleasure to make your acquaintance, Jim.

Jim (*leading them into the living-room*) Do come through. My wife's in the kitchen at the moment. A critical point in her preparations.

Nancy Well, I can certainly understand that! Can I help at all?

Jim I don't think so, thanks, I'm sure she's got everything under control.

An enormous clatter of falling saucepans is heard from the kitchen

Well, almost everything. She prefers to cope on her own.

Nancy In that case, perhaps you could excuse me for a minute. (*She dabs an eye with her handkerchief*) I have a problem with one of my lenses. May I go to your bathroom and fix it?

Jim Of course. Our bedroom's handiest, with the bathroom *en suite*. Then you can use my wife's dressing table, if you want to.

Nancy You're very kind. I suffer from myopia.

Jim leads Nancy across to bedroom A and opens the door

Jim Anything you need?

Nancy Only a new pair of eyeballs.

She disappears into the bedroom and shuts the door

Jim Bill, thank you very much for coming to see us.

Bill I like to visit with all my young executives in their homes. It's the only way to know a man's real character. And you're seen as a potential high-flyer, Jim.

Jim Well, thanks. What will you drink?

Bill Straight scotch for me. With a name like McGregor, what else would I drink?

Bill laughs heartily and Jim joins in

Jim (*pouring whisky for Bill*) I should have guessed. You have Scots forebears?

Bill I do indeed, sir, and proud of it. One of my ancestors killed five Englishmen at the Battle of Bannockburn.

Jim Oh. Well, no hard feelings. We were always good losers.

Bill My grandfather emigrated from Scotland in 1930. I'm entitled to wear the kilt.

Jim Then you'll be a good judge of whisky. I've a rather special malt here I'd like your opinion on. (*He hands Bill a drink*)

Bill That I'd be glad to give you. I'm mighty gratified to see Scottish
Distillers up six per cent today. On my advice, the New York office
bought four million shares last week.

Jim Ah, it's not for nothing they call you the Wall Street Wizard. Six
per cent, eh?

Bill That was an hour ago. They could be up further by now.

Jim I haven't had a chance to look at share prices since breakfast.

Bill (*slightly disapprovingly*) Well, don't let yourself get out of touch,
young man. Saturday's as important a day as any other in world
markets.

Jim Yes, of course. But I've been working all day on this month's
investment reports. They had to go to the States today.

Bill Sure, sure. Well, this is a great whisky you got here, Jim. I
congratulate you.

Jim I always say, no one makes scotch like the Scots.

Bill I won't drink any other.

Jim Well, it's good news about Scottish Distillers. Anything else
moving?

Bill Far East generally up one per cent.

Jim How about Yakohito?

Bill Up two point five.

Jim Excellent. We bought three million in London this week.

Bill Well done. New York should have done the same. I'll have to check
on that.

Jim I've been doing extensive research on Yakohito. They've brought
out this new interactive computer game. I think they're on a winner.

Bill Where d'you keep your terminal, Jim?

Jim It's in my study, down the corridor.

Bill There's a few prices I'd like to check before dinner.

We hear the kitchen door open

Edna emerges, and advances towards the men

Edna Evening, all.

Jim Ah ... er ... there you are, darling. (*He swallows hard*) Bill, this is
my wife, Edna.

Bill I'm mighty glad to make your acquaintance, Edna.

Edna grabs Bill's outstretched hand and shakes it vigorously

Edna Likewise, I'm sure. Hallelujah, brother!

Bill Oh, er ... Yeah, sure.

Edna Fight the good fight! Praise the Lord and keep the faith!

Bill (*a little baffled*) Yes, indeed. You're keen on religion, Edna?

Edna Oh yes, dead religious, I am. All my family are. My uncle was verger down the Reform Chapel. 'Til they caught him ——

Jim Edna! Is everything all right in the kitchen? I think I can smell something burning.

Edna Don't worry, that's just the oven hotting up. It hasn't been cleaned lately. (*To Bill*) My hubby tells me you're a religious person, Bill.

Bill That's true. I am a deacon of the American Church of the Holy Scripture. Religion is the cornerstone of my life.

Edna Oh, that's nice. Bit more religion's what we all need. 'Specially my nephews, it might keep them out of trouble. Do you know ——

Jim (*hastily*) Edna, what about a drink now?

Edna Not while I'm working, ta just the same. (*To Bill*) I see you got a drink then?

Bill That's right. Jim keeps a very fine whisky.

Edna Only I said to Jim, I said, I wonder if Mr McGregor drinks? 'Cause a lot of religious people are against it, aren't they?

Bill Some are, Edna, but our church has no objection to alcohol. After all, the good book says, "Take a little wine for thy health's sake."

Edna Does it? Cor blimey, my dad must be the healthiest bloke in our street! (*She gives a raucous laugh and digs her elbow into Bill's ribs*) Funny, his doctor's always saying the booze will kill him. But my dad don't believe him. He says he's seen more old drunks than old doctors!

Bill is somewhat taken aback, but puts it all down to British eccentricity

Bill We believe that the grape and the grain are gifts of the good Lord. We reserve our disapproval for lust and licentiousness! We hate wanton depravity!

Edna Yeah, that's the worst kind.

Bill We are with Moral Outrage, in its war on the permissive society. We believe in strict morality and family values. We oppose the tide of sexual laxity and indecency that threatens to engulf us!

Edna (*clapping briefly*) Hear, hear! Quite right. I think some of the stuff they put on telly these days is disgraceful! I often have to turn the sound down!

Bill I'm glad you agree, Edna. Jim knows that I expect the highest standard of moral behaviour from all my executives. Yes sir!

Jim Yes, indeed. You'll be glad to hear, Bill, that the *Sun* newspaper has now been banned from our London office.

Bill I'm not familiar with that publication.

Jim It often features pictures of undressed women.

Edna (*remembering*) Oh yes, I forgot to tell you! My niece Sharon, the one with the big chest, she's going to be in ——

Jim (*hastily*) Edna! Are you sure you won't have a drink?

Edna Yes, I really won't. If I start drinking on an empty tummy, sometimes my tongue runs away with me. Besides, I'd better get back to the kitchen. I just popped out to say how d'you do. (*She picks up the nibbles bowl and offers it to Bill*) Have a nibble, Bill?

Bill Thanks. (*Peering into the bowl*) Say, these are unusual. Some kinda nut?

Edna No, they're Whea ——

Jim Yes, they're specially processed for party food. Quite hard to come by, but we're rather fond of them.

Bill puts a handful into his mouth and chews them

Bill Yeah, these are good. My wife'll take the name from you, Edna. See if we can get them in the States. (*He notices something in the nibbles bowl*) Hey, what's that dark thing in there?

Jim Dark thing?

Bill Yeah. (*He pokes at the nibbles*) Looks like a hairpin!

Jim Yes. Yes, it does look like a hairpin, doesn't it? That's a … er … that's a humidifier. The metal attracts moisture, and keeps the nibbles cool and fresh.

Bill Smart idea. We must make sure we get one of those. Well, like I said, I'd like to look at your computer. There's some prices I need to update. And I want to buy some pharmaceutical stock, we're running short.

Jim Pharmaceuticals?

Bill I'm inclined to go for Hugo Toiletries.

Jim Hugo, yes. They're banking everything on their new perfume, Exotica. They've spent a fortune on promotion.

Edna Cor, don't put money on them, then. I've tried that Exotica, it's horrible. Makes you smell like a whore at a christening.

Bill You don't think it'll sell?

Edna Not a hope. All my friends hate it. If you want to back a winner, go for the firm that makes Primitive. That's what people like.

Bill Who markets Primitive, Jim?

Jim I think it's Lamasco. It'll be on their website.

Bill Any good?

Jim Small group, quite sound. Not very exciting in the past. They're better known for men's products.

Bill Is that so?

Jim Yes. They do Lionheart aftershave and body oil.

Edna Well, that's good stuff, an' all. My hubby likes me to rub him all over with it, after his bath on Sunday afternoon. Cor! That really gets him going! (*Remembering*) Doesn't it, Jim?

Jim Er … yes. Very stimulating.

Edna I'll say! (*Playfully*) He loves it when I do his tummy. (*She rubs Jim's midriff and gives one of her raucous laughs*)

Jim Edna, I'm sure Bill doesn't want to hear too many details of your … er, *our* private life.

Bill Don't be embarrassed, Jim. The pleasures of married life are a great source of strength to the busy executive. Well sir, I'm going to back your wife's judgment, buy a couple of million Lamasco, and see what happens.

Edna You'll be all right, you mark my words.

Bill Say Edna, you got any thoughts on detergents?

Edna Wham!

Bill Pardon me?

Edna Wham! That's the one. Gets all the beer stains out of my old man's shirts.

Jim (*hastily*) I don't get that many, Edna.

Edna (*realizing*) No. But if you did, Wham would get them out. It's the best. Everyone says so.

Bill Wham. Made by?

Jim Handel Brothers. North Country firm.

Bill Right. Guess I'll buy a few of those as well.

Jim Do you want to use the phone?

Bill No, I do all our buying and selling on the Internet now, it's quicker. Can we go check the prices?

Jim You go ahead. (*Pointing to the passage*) Into the passage there. The study's the last on the right. I just want a word with my wife. More scotch?

Bill Thanks. This is a real fine whisky.

Jim takes the bottle from the cabinet and fills Bill's glass

Edna More nibbles, Bill?

Bill Negative, thank you. I'll leave some for Nancy to try. (*As he goes; murmuring*) Lamasco, Handel Brothers. Sounds like a good double.

Bill exits to the study

The moment he's gone Jim grabs Edna's arm

Jim Edna, for God's sake! Will you stop trying to talk about your
dubious relatives? I don't want a wife with a criminal family!

Edna They're not criminals, Mr Watt. They're just unfortunate. They
haven't had the advantages in life what you've had.

Jim Well, please don't keep on about them. How's the dinner going?

Edna Not too well. It was hell, cutting that veg with your kitchen knife.
The handle's broke.

Jim It was broken, but I repaired it.

Edna Oh, it was you, was it? And what did you repair it with? Chewing
gum! Now the handle's come off, the veg is all ragged, and the gum's
somewhere in the cooking pot. Still, it's on now.

Jim This doesn't sound like a success, Edna. Just grill the steak and the
mushrooms, like I said.

Edna Certainly not. Tornadoes chassis I said I'd cook, and tornadoes
chassis I will cook. (*Heading to the kitchen*) But not if you keep me
stood here talking.

Edna exits and we hear the door close

At the same time we hear a key turn and the front door opens

*Helen enters, looking very glamorous. She's carrying an elegant
shopping bag from an expensive store, and a smaller, less expensive,
plastic bag. She swiftly closes the front door, puts the bags down and
hurls herself at Jim*

Helen Oh, Jim! Jim! I'm terribly sorry! What a rotten cow I've been!

Jim My God! Helen! What are you doing here?

Helen I live here, darling, and always will, as long as you want me!

Jim But ... but ...

Helen I got as far as the Savoy, and then the doorman looked like you,
and I realized I love you, and I couldn't let you down! Jim, say you
forgive me!

Jim Yes, yes, of course. But listen ——

Helen Don't worry, darling. I'll fix the meal. It's a bit late for tournedos,
but I've brought a Chinese takeaway. I'll dress it up to look special.
What time do the guests arrive?

Jim I'm trying to tell you, Helen, they're already here!

Helen (*looking round*) Here! Where?

Jim Bill's in the study, using the Internet. His wife's in the bathroom.

Helen Oh well, I'll say I was held up on the job.

Jim But listen, that's not all! Edna ——

Nancy appears from bedroom A

Nancy That's better. Gee, these lenses are a pain. I guess if God had intended us to fix double glazing in our eyes, he'd have given us square eyeballs.

Jim Ah, er, everything all right now, Nancy?

Nancy I reckon they'll hold for a couple of hours. (*Noticing Helen*) Say, this must be your wife.

Helen That's right, Mrs McGregor, I'm Helen. How do you do.

Nancy Hi. Delighted to make your acquaintances. And it's Nancy, please.

Helen Of course. I'm terribly sorry I'm late, Nancy. My photo shoot overran.

Nancy Oh? Jim said you were in the kitchen.

Helen Did he? Oh, that's so typical of Jim. The perfect husband, covering for his wife. He didn't want you to know I was late, so he started things off himself. I'll bet that's the truth, isn't it, Jim?

Jim Er, in a way. I certainly started something off. Nancy, what will you drink?

Nancy Oh, I guess a gin and tonic would hit the spot.

Jim G and T. Helen?

Helen The same, please.

During the following, Jim fixes the drinks and hands them out

Nancy Did you say a photo shoot, Helen? You must be a fashion model.

Helen That's right. We've been showing jewellery this afternoon.

Nancy How fascinating! Did you get to wear some fabulous things?

Helen Oh yes. I hated having to give them all back.

Nancy (*noticing*) Hey, you're not wearing your wedding ring! I hope you didn't hand that in, along with the other stuff!

Helen What? Er, no. No, I saw the danger of that, so I put it in a drawer before I went out.

Nancy Smart move. Gee, if I ever lost my wedding ring, my husband would never forgive me. Where is Bill, anyway?

Jim He's in the study, doing deals on the Internet.

Nancy Well, would you believe it? That guy just can't stop working! Buy this, sell that, borrow the other. You'd think all he cared about was money!

Jim Well, money's quite important in our job, Nancy.

Nancy Sure, but it isn't everything. Bill knows that. Deep inside, he's a very spiritual person. As I am. Faith, beauty, art, friendship — they're the really important things. Not money.

Jim Friendship is very important, yes.

Nancy (*remembering*) That reminds me, I got a tip this afternoon. Friendship Assurance is planning a bonus, their price will go up. I must let Bill know. You say he's on the Internet?

Jim In my study. It's this way. (*He leads her towards the rear passage and indicates the study*) At the end, on the right.

Nancy (*as she leaves*) If you'll excuse me, I'll tell Bill now, so he can buy cheap. The shares are going to rocket tonight.

Nancy exits

Helen sighs with relief

Helen Hooray, we've sorted that out. No problem.

Jim Helen, we have one hell of a problem. Edna Chapman is in the kitchen!

Helen God, you haven't brought her in to do the cooking? She did lunch here once. It came out like minced gumboot!

Jim Edna is doing the cooking. And, furthermore, she's posing as my wife!

Helen She's what?

Jim I had to have a wife for the evening, remember? Edna's doing the job for a fee.

Helen Edna! Are you out of your mind?

Jim Helen, I was desperate! Bill's already fired a French executive for living in sin! You'd gone, no one else would help, then Edna stepped in.

Helen Well, I'm here now. You can tell her to step out again.

Jim Not easy.

Helen Double her fee to give up the job.

Jim She might agree to that. But Bill's already met her. I introduced her as my wife.

Helen Oh my God! When you screw up, you really make a job of it!

Jim Don't moan at me! If you hadn't stormed out this morning, none of this would have happened!

Helen All right, I'm sorry, darling. I just want to make the evening a success for you. Tell Bill he must have misunderstood. Say Edna's the cook. No, the assistant cook. I'm taking over.

Jim I'd never swing that on Bill McGregor.

Helen You'll have to try. Don't forget, Nancy thinks *I'm* your wife. I'll bet he's easier to hoodwink than she is.

Jim (*thinking aloud*) Well, if I can get him excited about business ...

Helen Listen, I've bought a new dress to wear, I'll change in the bedroom. Take the Chinese meal to the kitchen, and tell Edna you'll double her money to quit.

Jim OK, I'll have a go.

Jim picks up the elegant shopping bag in error and exits to the kitchen. Oblivious, Helen takes the plastic bag with the Chinese meal and disappears into bedroom A. As the door closes, Bill and Nancy return from the study

Nancy You sure five million Friendship is enough?

Bill It is for now, I don't want to start a stampede.

Nancy Why did you buy that other company?

Bill Lamasco? Bill's wife had a hunch.

Nancy Oh, that was her idea, was it?

Bill Yeah. She has pretty strong views on perfume. Come to that, she has pretty strong views on most things. Yes sir, she looks kind of quaint, but she sure is quite a character.

Nancy Quaint? She looks fabulous!

Bill Fabulous? Jim's wife?

Nancy She's one of the most attractive women I've ever met. I wish I looked like her.

Bill Well, stand out in the rain for a month, and you might!

Nancy Bill, what are you saying? Jim's wife looks great! What about that hair? I'll make some notes, and have Benito do mine like that when we get home.

Bill You want to upset the neighbours?

Nancy Are you crazy? The hair's beautiful! The woman's beautiful! Did you know she's a fashion model?

Bill She's a model? What does she model for, umbrella handles? (*Looking around*) Where are they, anyway?

Nancy In the kitchen, I guess. Jim's so sweet. His wife was late in from her job, so he's helping with the cooking.

Bill Jim said she didn't like help.

Nancy Women can change their minds. Anyway, I'd say they have a pretty strong marriage.

Bill Well, that's what I demand from my executives. They're a mighty odd couple but, as long as that's what they want, that's their business.

Nancy Why do you say they're odd?

Bill (*looking around to check he won't be overheard*) Well, for one thing, she looks like Quasimodo on a bad night. For another, why do they keep disappearing and deserting their guests?

Nancy I told you, Jim's helping in the kitchen. Ah, here he comes.

Jim emerges from the rear passage looking harrassed

Jim Ah, there you are! Bill, did you get the Lamasco shares?

Bill Five million. At one-seventy-five.

Jim That's a good price.

Bill It is, if your wife's got it right. And Scottish Distillers are up another two points.

Jim Great! Congratulations, Bill! And that reminds me, more scotch?

Bill No thanks, I still have some.

Jim Another drink, Nancy?

Nancy Yes, I guess I could take the same again. But I feel I really should be helping. As your wife was late home.

Jim (*taking Nancy's glass and pouring a drink*) No, no, there's no need. She has her own way of doing things. She hates help.

Bill But you were helping her just now.

Jim Was I? Er, no. No, no, I wasn't. I was just encouraging her. "Well done, dear! Keep it up!" That sort of thing. She doesn't mind having me there, because I don't know what I'm doing. She wouldn't like having another cook around. Say when.

Jim pours tonic into Nancy's glass but, in his anxious state, his hand shakes and he pours tonic on her wrists as well

Oh! Oh Nancy, I'm sorry.

Nancy It doesn't matter, it's only tonic. Still I guess I'd better wash it off, it dries kinda sticky. If you'll excuse me, I'll just slip back to the bathroom.

She puts her glass down and moves towards bedroom A

Jim Right. (*Realizing Helen is in there*) Er, no! Don't go in there! That bathroom's out of action!

Nancy Out of action? It was OK ten minutes ago.

Jim Yes, but it's temperamental. I washed my hands just now, and the water wouldn't run away.

Bill Probably an airlock. Shall I try and fix it?

Bill advances towards bedroom A. Jim darts round and gets between the McGregors and the bedroom door

Jim No, no, there's another bathroom by the study. (*He looks quickly at his watch and feigns huge surprise*) Good Lord! It's seven fifty-three!

Bill Yeah? So what?

Jim The Borneo Stock Exchange has just opened. We ought to check what that's done to our shares.

Bill In Borneo?

Jim The Far East's so volatile at present. We may need to sell in a hurry.

Bill (*alarmed*) You could be right, at that. OK, let's go see.

Jim And Nancy can use the main bathroom, it's just by the study.

Nancy Sure, if you say so.

Jim shepherds them towards the rear passage but before he gets there, he draws back

Jim Look, you two go on ahead. I promised to warn my wife when it's five to eight. Something coming to the boil.

Bill OK, as long as you don't try to help her. (*He gives a hearty laugh*) I'll let you know what's happening in the market.

Nancy Jim, you're a saint.

Jim is ushering them out as the door to bedroom A partially opens

Bill and Nancy exit into the rear passage

Helen's head appears from behind the bedroom door. She looks round, to check the coast is clear, and then emerges, wearing only a bra and panties. She's halfway across the room, making for the kitchen, when Jim turns round and sees her. She stops by the sofa

Jim (*horrified*) Helen! What the hell are you doing?

Helen You stole my bloody dress, didn't you! I've got to get it back!

Jim I stole your dress?

Helen You took the wrong bag, you stupid oaf! Left me to dress up in chop suey and egg fried rice!

Jim Look, we've no time for games! What are you saying?

Helen You gave me the Chinese meal, and took the bag with my dress! And I need it!

Jim You certainly do! Models are used to walking around like that, but you'd give Bill McGregor a heart attack!

Helen So fetch my goddamn dress! It'll be in the kitchen, won't it? Just go and get it!

Jim I can't go in there now!

Helen Well, if you can't, I can!

Helen advances towards the kitchen. Jim stops her

Jim No, Helen! No!

Helen Why the hell can't we go in the kitchen? It's our sodding flat, isn't it?

Jim Edna's in there, and she's angrier than a trapped ferret! Put your old dress back on!

Helen The old dress is torn down the middle. My heel caught when I took it off.

Jim Oh, my God!

Helen What's Edna on about, anyway? You gave her money, didn't you?

Jim She agreed to hand over the job for three hundred pounds. But her pride's hurt.

Helen So what?

Jim So if we go in there, there'll be a shouting match. And if the McGregors come out and hear it, I'm ruined!

Helen What about the dinner?

Jim That's only half-ruined. She was cooking the veg in a glass dish, and it cracked down the middle. She's trying to find another one, and scooping the veg off the floor!

Helen Oh hell! Well, get her out of there, and let me take over!

Jim You can't play hostess in your underwear!

Helen Well, get the bloody dress then!

Jim (*bracing up*) All right, I suppose I'll have to. But you get back in the bedroom. And be quick!

Helen OK.

As Helen turns back towards the bedroom, Bill is heard calling back to Nancy as he leaves the study

Bill (*off*) OK, Nancy, keep an eye on it for me. I'll be back.

Jim (*pushing Helen behind the sofa, out of sight*) Oh God! There's no time! Quick, get down!

Bill (*off; approaching*) Hey Jim, we're riding high! Scottish Distillers are still going up, and now Handel Brothers are on the move!

Bill enters

Jim (*advancing on Bill to keep him away from the sofa*) Well, that's great news!

Bill Borneo's given us a boost. We're way ahead of the pack.

Jim Borneo's a key market these days.

Bill Nancy's keeping an eye on things. I'm here for another scotch.

Jim (*refilling Bill's glass*) Good.

Bill Handel's one of your wife's hunches. That's a shrewd business-woman you've got there. And she cooks as well!

Jim Yes. But rather slowly.

Bill No hurry, I'm enjoying the whisky.

Helen lets out a strangled sneeze from behind the sofa

Bless you!

Jim Thank you. (*He takes out his handkerchief and blows his nose loudly*)

Bill (*slightly accusing*) You haven't got a cold, I hope.

Jim No, no, it's just the bubbles in the tonic. Why don't you take Nancy another drink?

Bill Negative. She takes too many, her ears go red. Say, you seem kinda nervous.

Jim Nervous? Me? Good heavens, no. Why don't you nib another hubble ... er, have another nibble? Er, have another drink?

Bill Jim, you just poured me one!

Helen lets out another strangled sneeze from behind the sofa. This time Bill is focused

Hey! There's someone behind that sofa!

Jim No, I don't think so. There wasn't, last time I looked.

Bill But I heard a noise!

Jim Mice! We have a lot of trouble with mice!

Bill That was a sneeze! Mice don't sneeze!

Jim British mice do. It's the damp climate.

Bill Are you crazy? There's a human person behind that sofa, I swear it! It could be a burglar. I'll take a look.

Jim No! If there's any danger, it's better for me to look! We can't risk one of our top men. Now let's see ... (*He walks over, looks behind the sofa, and reacts with mild surprise*) Good Lord, you're right! There is someone here. It's ... er ... well, it's Helen.

Bill Helen? Who's Helen?

Helen's head appears above the back of the sofa. The rest of her remains out of sight

Helen I am. Hello.

Bill Who are you?

Jim She's Helen.

Bill Yes, but who is she? What's she doing here?

Helen I'm Jim's wi ——

Jim She's my wife's cleaning lady.

Bill Cleaning lady?

Jim Yes. She's the lady who does our cleaning.

Helen (*adapting quickly and attempting a cockney accent*) That's right, guv'nor. Pleased to meet you. Ten years I've been doing for his missis. A real lady, she is. Cor blimey, yes!

Jim We need domestic help, you see, because we're both working.

Bill Yes, but where did she suddenly spring from? And what's she doing here at this time?

Jim A good question. Well, two good questions, actually. Helen, where did you suddenly spring from? And what are you doing here at this time?

Helen I'm dusting.

Bill Dusting?

Helen Behind the sofa, yeah. It's real dusty back here. No wonder I keep sneezing! Strewth!

Bill Why are you down on the floor?

Helen I've got to dust by hand. The hoover broke. Some string got caught in it.

Jim Helen's working late today. Her cleaning was held up, because she was helping my wife with the cooking.

Bill I thought your wife wouldn't accept help with the cooking.

Jim Like I said, she doesn't mind encouragement from people who aren't any good at it. Helen's as useless as I am. Aren't you, Helen?

Helen Worse. Anyway, I remembered I hadn't cleaned this bit behind the sofa, so I popped in here to finish it off.

Jim Helen's tremendously conscientious. Works all hours. A model employee.

Bill (*half-convinced*) Well, you certainly must be, young lady. You'd better stand up and take a bow.

Helen Ta, I'm sure.

Helen is about to stand up but Jim hastily puts his hands on her shoulders and pushes her down

Jim Not now, Helen. Mr McGregor was only joking. Just concentrate on finishing the job. We don't want you working too late.

Helen disappears from view

Nancy hurries in, full of excitement

Nancy Bill, what was that perfume business you bought into?

Bill Lamasco.

Nancy I thought so! They've just shot up twelve points!

Bill Twelve points! Wow! You sure you got that right?

Nancy Yes! This perfume of theirs, Primitive — France just voted it Smell of the Year!

Bill Jim, your wife's a genius! First Handel's, now Lamasco! Tell her from me! She's a genius!

Jim Thanks, I will.

Nancy They're still rising! Big orders from Europe!

Bill (*moving off towards the study*) Jeepers! This I've got to see! Excuse me a minute.

Bill exits

Nancy glances surreptitiously at her watch. She's hungry

Nancy Bill tells me you got some swell nibbles.

Jim Oh yes, he seems to like them. Would you care to try some? (*He proffers the bowl and Nancy takes some*)

Nancy I certainly would. This investing's a hungry business. (*Tasting the nibbles*) Yeah, these eats are kind of cute. Unusual. Yet I guess I've seen them before some place.

Jim Perhaps you've been to dinner at the Palace?

Nancy (*awed*) No. I've not yet had that honour.

Jim Her Majesty always serves these with cocktails.

Nancy Gee!

Jim But I expect you've come across them at one of London's more exclusive parties.

Nancy I guess so. I must get the details from your wife. Are you sure I shouldn't be helping her?

Jim Positive. I'm sorry dinner's a little delayed, due to her getting home late.

Nancy I'm sure she's mighty brave, entertaining guests after a hard day's work. (*Looking around*) Well, you have a very comfortable flat here. I just love your sofa.

Jim (*alarmed*) Oh good. We're rather fond of it. We use it a lot. For sitting down, and so on.

Nancy It's such an attractive colour. What sort of fabric is that?

Nancy advances to inspect the sofa more closely. Jim gets between Nancy and the sofa, carrying the bowl of nibbles

Jim More nibbles, Nancy? You must be famished.

Nancy (*taking some nibbles*) Thanks. I was saying, what's that delightful fabric on your sofa?

Nancy tries to sidestep Jim for a closer look, but he is in the way again

Jim Ah, well … That's a sort of sofa fabric. We use it in Britain for putting on furniture. Sofas, and so on. I shouldn't get too close to it, it's just been spring cleaned.
Nancy Well, I wasn't going to dirty it.
Jim No no, I didn't mean that. It's just that I think the cleaning fluid was a little strong. It was making my wife sneeze earlier.
Nancy So we can't use the sofa this evening?
Jim Oh yes, we can! Later! The covers just need time to breathe.
Nancy The sofa covers are breathing?
Jim Well, you know, they have to settle down. Lose the strong smell. They only came back from the cleaners this afternoon.
Nancy Gee, you had the sofa spring cleaned for our visit!
Jim Well, since you ask, yes. Nothing but the best for our American friends.
Nancy I sure appreciate that. Oh well, if I can't help, I guess I'll get back to the computer. This trading's kind of addictive. (*She moves off towards the study*)
Jim Tell Bill dinner won't be long.
Nancy He'll be mighty glad to hear that.

Nancy disappears into the rear passage

Jim hurries to the sofa and leans over

Jim Quick, Helen! Come out of there!

Helen emerges, somewhat indignant

Helen You stupid birdbrain! Why did you say I was the cleaning lady? We agreed Edna would quit, and I'd be your wife!
Jim Why did you have to sneeze? Once he'd seen you, we couldn't get away with that!
Helen Why not?
Jim Because he'd never accept my wife was hiding behind the sofa in her underwear! Especially when he'd just heard she was busy in the kitchen!
Helen Great. So Bill thinks the cleaning lady's your wife, and his wife thinks your girlfriend's the cleaning lady!

Jim And I think that I'm in the soup! Without a snorkel!

Helen And that's not all!

Jim My God! There's more?

Helen There's worse. What do we tell Nancy when she runs into Edna? It's bound to happen.

Jim We agreed to say Edna's the cleaning lady.

Helen We can't do that now. Bill thinks I'm the cleaning lady.

Jim Two cleaning ladies?

Helen Not very likely. And he might think they were overpaying you!

Jim Oh hell! Hell and damnation! Perhaps I should just cut my throat.

Helen Don't panic! We'll say Edna's a neighbour who's just popped in.

Jim But Edna would deny it.

Helen Say she's a barmy neighbour who talks nonsense. Someone we try to help.

Jim Pray it doesn't come to that. Now, for God's sake, get dressed! You may have to go back to the Savoy.

A disgruntled Edna comes from the kitchen, carrying the dress bag

Edna I don't know what's going on here. What's this dress doing in my kitchen?

Jim (*grabbing the bag*) Ah, thank heavens! That's Miss Foster's dress! Quick, Helen, get into this, and stay out of sight! Now move!

Helen (*taking the bag and hurrying to bedroom A; to Jim*) You'd better come, and we'll work out a plan.

Jim In a minute. I've got to talk to Edna first.

Helen Be quick. I guess we'll just have to bluff it out.

Helen exits to bedroom A and shuts the door

Jim Edna, what on earth's happening with the dinner?

Edna It's all gone wrong. A right pig's ear. I can't find another dish for the veg, the chewing gum's stuck to the carrots, and the steak's still frozen. Oh, and the recipe fell on the hotplate and burned.

Jim Dear God, what are we going to do?

Edna I was distracted, you see, with all this confusion.

Jim I told you to keep it simple.

Edna Well, that's what I'm going to do now. I'll save my tornadoes chassis for another time, and give them a nice hotpot.

Jim Is there time for that?

Edna Yes, I found an old pressure cooker in the cupboard. I'll bung the lot in there, it'll be done in twenty minutes!

Jim I hope so. I do hope so. But we'll have to put something on the table soon, Bill's wife is starving. (*Remembering*) The melon! That's it! Put the melon out, quick!

Edna And what about that little word "please"? Now I'm not your wife any more, I'm entitled to a little respect!

Jim Yes, yes, sorry. Please put the melon out.

Edna That's more like it. Melon coming up.

Edna exits to the kitchen

Jim (*to himself*) Today's a day I should have stayed in bed.

Jim pours himself another gin and is gulping it down

Nancy returns from the study, carrying an empty glass

Nancy Bill's asking for a refill, Jim. Right now I can't tear him away from the screen.

Jim (*taking the glass from Nancy and pouring whisky*) My pleasure, Nancy. Does that mean it's still good news?

Nancy You bet. He's sitting there, as pleased as a monkey on a peanut farm.

During the following, Edna enters from the kitchen with two melon portions, which she puts on the dinner table

Jim Bill's a very shrewd operator, you know. And an innovator. He's done a lot for Wilson Keppel since he took over.

Nancy (*watching Edna with surprise; preoccupied*) Yes?

Jim The great thing is, he's receptive to new ideas.

Nancy Yes?

Jim As a matter of fact, there are a couple of suggestions I want to put to him, while he's here.

Nancy Yes?

Jim Yes. The market changes so fast these days. One always has to be prepared for the unexpected.

Edna exits to the kitchen

Nancy Sure. Yes. The unexpected. Say, I hope I don't seem nosey, but who was that?

Jim Who was what?

Nancy A woman just came in and put melon on the table.

Jim Oh ... ah ... that must have been Mrs Chapman.

Nancy Mrs Chapman?

Jim Yes. Our next door neighbour. She likes to come in and help.

Nancy I thought your wife didn't accept help.

Jim Well, Mrs Chapman's an exception. A very lonely woman. On her own all day. Popping in here gives her an outing, so my wife puts up with her.

Nancy She didn't say anything. And what's happened to her hair?

Jim Don't ask. I'm afraid Mrs Chapman's a little strange. Helping here is therapy for her. She needs to feel needed.

Nancy Well, it's mighty good of you both to go along with that.

Jim If she does speak, she may not make much sense. (*He points a finger at his brain and turns it*) We just try to humour her. Makes her feel good.

Nancy Of course. I understand.

Edna enters with two more melon portions

Jim Thank you, Mrs Chapman. We're very grateful.

Edna So you should be. I got the chewing gum off the veg. And I've put the water pistol in the breadbin.

Nancy (*aside; to Jim*) Poor woman!

Jim Ah, thank you very much. Good thinking.

Nancy (*gushing*) Mr Watt was just telling me what an enormous help you are, Mrs Chapman. He says they'd never manage without you.

Edna That's true enough. If I didn't come in regular, this place would be like a council tip.

Nancy I'm sure. Say, what lovely melon! Jim, isn't that just the most beautiful melon you ever saw?

Jim Yes. Yes, it does look like very good melon.

Nancy Bill and I just adore melon.

Edna I prefer prawn cocktail myself. But I can only serve what I'm given.

Nancy I guess that's all any of us can do. Well, I'd better take this drink back to the boss. Lovely to meet you, Mrs Chapman. Keep up the good work.

Nancy exits to the study

Edna Is that the American bloke's wife?

Jim Yes. Nancy McGregor. A very pleasant person.

Edna A bit strange, if you ask me. All that fuss about a bit of melon. Oh well, perhaps they don't get much fruit in America. I suppose Miss Foster's going to be your wife now, is she?

Jim I'm not sure. There may be another change of plan. We've got to work something out. (*Hurrying to bedroom A and opening the door*) If you see Bill or Nancy, just talk about business. Or better still, don't say anything.

Jim disappears into bedroom A and shuts the door

Edna (*to herself*) Charming! And me slaving all night in a hot kitchen!

As Edna turns to go back to the kitchen, the doorbell rings. Edna goes to the hall and opens the front door

Terri Pringle is there. She holds a carrier bag and is wearing her glasses

Terri Hello again.
Edna Oh yes, you're the young lady from Mr Watt's office.
Terri (*bursting in*) That's right. He wanted my help this evening. I thought I wasn't free, but I am, because the director's got a migraine.
Edna Oh. That's nice.
Terri I'm going to be Mr Watt's hostess tonight.
Edna Oh yes? He said there'd been a change of plan.
Terri I've brought my best dress. Can I change in the bedroom?
Edna I expect so. (*Indicating the door of bedroom B*) Better use that one. There's no one there, as far as I know.
Terri (*opening the bedroom door*) Ta. Don't tell him I'm here. It's to be a big surprise.
Edna I'm sure it will be.

Terri goes into bedroom B and shuts the door behind her

Bill comes bustling on, full of enthusiasm, carrying a half-full glass of whisky

Bill Say, this is just astounding! (*Noticing Jim's absence*) Hey! Where's Jim?
Edna He's in the bedroom.
Bill Oh? Freshening up, I guess. Listen, those tips you gave me are red hot! Lamasco's up fifteen points, and Handel Brothers up twenty!
Edna Oh, that's nice. You can't go wrong backing quality, that's what I always say.
Bill Well, keep on saying it! We made a hundred thousand bucks in half an hour!

Edna We did?
Bill Yeah, the firm did. That'll mean a bonus for Jim, which no doubt
he'll share with you. Did he tell you you're a genius, Mrs Watt?
Edna No, he didn't, and I'm not.
Bill You're not a genius?
Edna No, I'm not Mrs Watt.
Bill What?
Edna I'm not Mrs Watt.
Bill You're not? But I don't understand. Jim said you were his wife.
Edna I was going to be. But after I did what he wanted, he changed his
mind.
Bill What?
Edna I'm just his skivvy now.
Edna You're with him and you're not married? That's appalling! This
is the sort of thing that's rotting our society!

Nancy enters, excited

Nancy They're still rising! Lamasco's hit two-twenty!
Bill Nancy, can you believe this? This lady isn't married to Jim!
Nancy Of course I believe it. I've met Jim's wife.
Bill I thought I had. But they're not legit.
Nancy Who aren't?
Bill Jim and his wife. They're not married!
Nancy Of course they are. I've met her.

*Jim and Helen emerge from bedroom A, determinedly bright, having
decided to bluff it out. Helen's in her new dress*

Jim Now then, everyone, another drink before dinner?
Helen I hope you all like melon.
Nancy And here she is! Helen, you look fabulous!
Helen Thank you, Nancy.
Bill You're crazy, Nancy! This woman's the cleaning lady!
Nancy Huh! Some cleaning lady!
Jim You've misunderstood, Bill. Edna here is our cleaning lady.
Nancy You said she was your neighbour.
Jim Yes. It's very convenient. She comes in from next door to clean
for us.
Bill Don't give me that. I know what she is. And you should be ashamed
of yourself! (*Indicating Helen*) This is your cleaning lady! I saw this
woman behind the sofa. Dusting and sneezing. Because of the string
in the hoover.

Nancy Bill, you're not making any sense! You've had too much scotch again!

Bill Listen, I saw her with my own eyes!

Jim Ah, perhaps your lenses let you down. Actually it was Edna you saw.

Bill I don't have any goddamn lenses! It's my wife who has the myopia!

Jim Well, you never know, it can be catching.

Bill Young man, I don't know what trick you're trying to pull. But I'll remind you, you introduced Edna here as your wife.

Jim I'm sorry, Bill, you must have misheard. Perhaps I said, she's a great help to my wife.

Bill And a great help to *you*, from the sound of it! She said she sees you in the bath! (*To Edna*) Isn't that true?

Edna Well yes, of course, I do see him in his bath. We're very broad-minded here. If he's still in the bath when I come to it, I just carry on.

Bill So it seems. You rub lotions into his body!

Edna (*exasperated*) Look, I'm a working woman, I just try to earn my money.

Bill Sodom and Gomorrah! He *pays* you?

Edna When he remembers.

Bill This is unbelievable! What's going on here?

Nancy Bill, calm down. You know what your doctor said. The fact is, you've got these two ladies mixed up.

Jim indicates Edna and Helen, who stand close together and look totally different

Jim Easily done. They are very similar, aren't they?

Bill Baloney! Nancy, God knows what they've been telling you, but it's clear to me this man's involved in a web of sin. Some sort of sordid triangle! The woman Edna is his mistress. I daren't guess where this other one fits in.

Helen (*brightly*) Good. Well, shall we all sit down to dinner? Bill, would you like to say grace?

Bill No, I would not! And we shall not sit down to dinner! I would not dine in this den of iniquity if I were starving! We shall leave at once!

Edna But what about my hotpot?

Bill Confound your hotpot, woman, we are leaving!

Jim Better put it on anyway, Edna. The rest of us have to eat. And Mr McGregor might change his mind.

Edna Right. I'll get on with it then. (*As she goes to the kitchen; grumbling*) No sense in wasting good food, even if some people do have money to throw around like drunken sailors.

Edna exits and we hear the kitchen door shut

Bill I shall not change my mind, sir! I can tell you, Watt, I'm horrified
at your behaviour. I shall see you in your office on Monday, to discuss
your future, if any. You know that I demand high moral principles
from all my staff.

Jim I do know that, Mr McGregor, and I apologize for all the confusion.
I assure you that I do have high moral principles. This has all been a
complete misunderstanding.

Bill Yeah? Like Pearl Harbour was a misunderstanding!

Jim Yes. I'd like you to know that I am romantically involved with only
one young lady. And there she is!

*Jim points at Helen, who is standing by the door of bedroom B. That
door is now flung open, and Terri Pringle appears, in a stunning low
cut evening dress, and without her glasses*

Terri Jim darling, great news! I don't have to do *The Naked Dance*
tonight. So I can spend the night with you after all!

Everyone else is astonished

I'll do everything you wanted, Jim. I'll be the best little wife you ever
had!

*With outstretched arms, Terri advances towards the nearest male figure,
who happens to be Bill. Without her glasses, she stumbles and dislodges
the top of her gown and falls against Bill, knocking his whisky down the
front of his suit*

The Lights fade to Black-out

SCENE 2

The same. Ten minutes later

*Only Bill and Helen are onstage. Bill sits grumpily in a chair, drinking
a fresh glass of scotch. Helen is trying to sponge the old whisky off his
suit with a damp cloth*

Helen Gosh, Mr McGregor, you've certainly done well with those
shares. Jim says all your selections are up more than thirty per cent!

Bill (*surly*) Yeah. So at least I can afford a new suit.

Helen That shouldn't be necessary, the stain's coming out all right. I'm using that cleaning stuff Edna recommended. It's magic!

Bill Is that so. Pity she couldn't use it to clean up her act. Anything happening on that taxi yet?

Helen Jim's phoning from the study. I must say, Edna did you a favour with those tips, didn't she?

Bill Yeah, I have to admit that. Listen, now I know all the facts, I don't blame any of you girls. You were trying to help out a friend — that's a Christian act. I reserve my wrath for your paramour. He's the villain here.

Helen Oh, Jim's not a bad chap, really.

Bill Not bad? He lures an innocent young girl like you into cohabitation! And then he hasn't the decency to make an honest woman of you!

Helen Don't worry, I'm still working on that.

Bill Then he persuades three foolish young women to try and deceive his boss! That's not the kind of behaviour Wilson Keppel expects from our managers. The man's a limb of Satan!

Jim enters from the study

Jim I finally got through to the cab firm. They say fifteen minutes. It's a busy time.

Bill And an incompetent limb at that!

Jim Mr McGregor, when you talk about incompetence, I'd like to say that I have run the London office successfully for two years. And, during the course of this evening, we've made some very successful deals.

Bill We can thank that Edna broad for those. Once I've got rid of you, I may hire her instead.

Helen (*giving Bill's suit a final wipe*) I think that's the best I can do. It should be OK when it dries.

Bill I certainly hope so.

Helen (*as she goes*) I'll see how Edna's getting on in the kitchen.

Helen exits

Jim Mr McGregor, I must remind you, we have employment laws in this country. You'll find it difficult to fire a man just for being unmarried.

Bill You reckon? Listen, Watt, there are ways and means of getting rid of people. There's a vacancy in our Kabul office. I tried to fill it last week, but the guy resigned instead.

Jim Oh. Yes. I heard about that.

Bill You might feel the same way. The fact is, our firm has the Moral Outrage account, and the Church of the Holy Scripture account. I'm not about to risk losing those by having a proven philanderer running our UK branch!

Nancy returns from the study

Nancy They're still rising, Bill! Lamasco's up forty per cent! There's talk of a takeover.

Jim Surely that should count for something, Mr McGregor. Your visit here has earned you a great deal of money.

Bill Money isn't everything, young man. Morality, decency, fair dealing — those are the important things. Nancy, get back on the net and sell ninety per cent of tonight's shares. And make sure you screw a good price out of some poor sucker before they all go down again.

Nancy Sell ninety per cent?

Bill Yeah. Let ten per cent ride, in case they go up again.

Nancy I don't know how to deal on the terminal here.

Jim All right, Nancy, I'll come with you. And I'll chase up that taxi.

Terri enters from bedroom B. She's now back to her day clothes and is wearing her glasses

Terri Mr Watt, could you call a cab for me, please? And I'm very sorry I embarrassed you.

Jim Don't worry, Terri, I was pretty embarrassed already. Excuse me, we'd better get those deals done.

Jim and Nancy exit to the study

Terri (*to Bill*) And I'm sorry I embarrassed you, as well.

Bill I guess you thought you were acting for the best. I've already said, I don't blame you misguided young women. You were exploited by that wicked lecher.

Terri Oh, Jim's not a bad man, really.

Bill Young women keep telling me that! Does he have it written on his bedroom ceiling?

Terri (*sadly*) He thinks you might fire him from the firm.

Bill He thinks right. I cannot have the good name of Wilson Keppel tarnished by gross moral turpitude.

Terri He's very good at his job.

Bill How would you know that?

Terri Well, I work for Wilson Keppel, don't I?

Bill Do you indeed? I didn't know that.

Terri I'm in Accounts. Terri Pringle.

Bill Is that so? Then I'm afraid I need to think again about your scandalous behaviour. I may have to consider your position.

Terri You were very happy with my position the Christmas before last.

Bill I beg your pardon?

Terri I recognize you now. You're Bill McGregor, the big boss from the States, aren't you?

Bill Mr McGregor to you, young woman.

Terri That's something else that was different last time we met.

Bill You're saying we've met before?

Terri That's right. When I worked in the New York office. The year before last.

Bill And we had some personal contact?

Terri Right on. At the Christmas party.

Bill (*cautiously*) Oh. The Christmas party. We have had to discontinue that, I'm afraid.

Terri What a shame! Why was that then?

Bill It was degenerating into a rabble. I'm not against alcohol in principle, Miss Pringle. But some of the junior staff were indulging to excess.

Terri You're right there! Most of them were drinking like they had hollow legs!

Bill Yeah. And a lot of them don't have the spunk to hold their liquor like older men. And the problem wasn't just drink. I'm afraid there were cases of lewd behaviour.

Terri You can say that again! This junior broker trapped me in the restroom and tried to get my blouse off!

Bill That's terrible!

Terri He was aiming to have his wicked way with me!

Bill Disgraceful! That's why I had to put a stop to those functions! (*With prurient interest*) What happened next?

Terri This senior man came in and pulled the broker off me.

Bill I'm mighty relieved to hear that.

Terri Then the senior man took me into the executive sauna, and he had his wicked way with me.

Bill What? That's appalling! I apologize on behalf of the firm, Miss Pringle. I confess I was not fully cognisant of what was going on that night.

Terri (*giggling*) You were as drunk as a skunk, weren't you?

Bill Certainly not. I was a little dazed, because some jerk had laced my drink with a Mickey Finn. But it's not too late, Miss Pringle. It should still be possible to identify the man who assaulted you.

Terri Well, it wasn't an assault really. I quite enjoyed it.
Bill I'm shocked to hear that!
Terri And there's no problem identifying the man. It was you.

Bill, who was sipping his drink, gives a violent start and pours whisky down the front of his suit again

Bill What?
Terri Oh dear, that suit's unlucky, isn't it?
Bill Me? How dare you! That's not possible!
Terri Of course it was possible. You were younger then.
Bill I don't believe it! No one would!
Terri They would if I told them I'd seen your birthmark.
Bill (*clapping his hand to his groin; horrified*) My birthmark? You know about my birthmark?
Terri Also, my friend Kelly took a picture as we came out of the sauna. She's a proper little mischief-maker, is Kelly.
Bill A photograph!
Terri It's all right, your birthmark wasn't showing. But we were still a bit … you know … tangled up.
Bill This is a nightmare!
Terri Funny, you seemed to like it at the time. Don't worry, I'm not one of your kiss-and-tell floosies. I told Kelly to burn the picture.
Bill Thank God for that.
Terri But, knowing her, I'll bet she's kept the negative. She's a great one for souvenirs. Always has been.

Bill puts his head in his hands for a moment

Bill Young woman, you realize that if that photo got into the wrong hands — or if you told this story to anyone else — it would ruin me, and my marriage, and possibly Wilson Keppel?
Terri Right. And I wouldn't want that. Any more than I'd want Mr Watt to be sacked for gross moral turpentine.
Bill Oh, I get it. You're hoping if you keep quiet about New York, it'll persuade me to forget about tonight!
Terri Persuade is an ugly word, Mr McGregor. Let's just call it blackmail.
Bill (*sighing*) Well, you got a deal. I guess I was kind of hasty, anyway. "Forgive us our trespasses" the good book says. Sometimes we tend to forget that.

Jim and Nancy return from the study

Jim The deals are done, Mr McGregor. The profits are safe.

Nancy Jim's a very smart operator, Bill. He got top prices. Are you sure you want to lose his services?

Bill No, Nancy, I changed my mind about that. Miss Pringle here has been telling me what a great manager he is.

Nancy (*enthusiastically*) I'm sure she's right!

Bill And I guess we've all got to be more tolerant.

Nancy I keep telling you that, Bill.

Bill Besides, the way Helen operates, I dare say she might even make an honest man of him.

Jim Does that mean I keep my job?

Bill It does, Jim. On one condition.

Jim What's that?

Bill You hire your friend Edna as consultant. With her know-how, we shan't need market research. OK?

Jim If the fee's right, Bill, I'm sure she could be persuaded.

Bill Swell. Draw up a contract on Monday.

Jim Certainly. And I've got a condition, too.

Bill Let's hear it.

Jim I want Miss Pringle promoted to be my personal assistant.

Bill You got it.

Jim I think she can be a great help.

Bill She's helped you a lot already, Jim. More than you'll ever know. OK with you, Terri?

Terri You bet!

The phone rings. Jim picks up the receiver

Jim (*into the phone*) Hello? ... Oh, thank you. (*To Bill*) The taxi's here.

Bill Hell, who needs a taxi? We haven't had dinner yet!

Nancy (*pleased*) Oh Bill! You mean, we can stay?

Bill I guess so. We've got to eat some place.

Jim (*into the phone*) Sorry, that cab's not needed now. ... Yes, of course, put it on my account. Thanks. (*He replaces the receiver*)

Helen enters from the kitchen

Helen Right. We need to know how many for dinner.

Jim (*looking around*) I make it six, darling. Including Edna and Terri. Bill and Nancy have decided to stay.

Helen Hooray! That is good news!

Jim And that's not all. You might like to know, I'm keeping my job.

Helen Thank God. I wouldn't want you hanging around at home all day, playing with your water pistol. Right, that's six for dinner then. If you'd like to go to table, everyone, there's melon for starters. And then Edna's done us a delicious hotpot.

A loud bang is heard from the kitchen

Bill My God, what was that?
Nancy World War III?
Jim Whatever it was, it didn't sound like good news.

Edna enters from the kitchen. Her front is covered with wet stew and bits of vegetable and diced carrots are sticking to her forehead

Edna Sorry, everyone, there's no hotpot. The pressure cooker just exploded.
Helen Oh dear. Chop suey, anyone? ... Sweet and sour pork? ... Chicken noodles? (*She continues to ad-lib Chinese dishes*)

The Lights fade to Black-out

CURTAIN

FURNITURE AND PROPERTY LIST

ACT I
SCENE 1

On stage: Arch leading to a small hall and the front door
Passage leading to a kitchen, study and bathroom
Two bedroom doors
Long window with a windowsill. *On it*: phone
Sofa
Coffee table
Dining table. *On it*: vase of flowers
Drinks cabinet. *In it*: glasses, red wine, white wine, whisky, gin
and tonic

Off stage: Tray with two glasses of water, Wheatipuffs box with a loaded
water pistol inside, toast, milk, breadboard, cutlery, napkins, etc.
(**Helen**)
Two cups of tea (**Helen**)
Two refilled cups of tea (**Helen**)
Small holdall (**Helen**)

Personal: **Jim**: watch

SCENE 2

Off stage: Hoover (**Edna**)
Duster, polish spray (**Edna**)
Slim briefcase containing sheaf of papers, pen (**Terri**)
Fruit juice, can of beer, glass (**Jim**)
Notebook, pen (**Jim**)

Personal: **Edna**: cigarette end
Terri: glasses
Jim: handkerchief

ACT II
SCENE 1

Set: Cutlery and placemats on the dining table
Chewing gum under the dining table

Strike: Glasses of water, tea cups, Wheatipuffs, toast, milk, breadboard,
            cutlery, napkins, etc.

Off stage: Cruet, bottle opener (**Jim**)
            Small glass bowl containing Wheatipuffs, hairpin (**Edna**)
            Elegant shopping bag, plastic bag containing Chinese takeaway
              food and menu (**Helen**)
            Two servings of melon portions (**Edna**)
            Carrier bag (**Terri**)

Personal: **Nancy**: handkerchief, watch
            Jim: handkerchief
            Terri: glasses

SCENE 2

On stage: Glass of scotch (**Bill**)
            Damp cloth (**Helen**)

Personal: **Terri**: glasses

LIGHTING PLOT

Practical fittings required: hoover power point

ACT I
SCENE 1

To open: Interior lighting. Sunlight streams through the US window

Cue 1	**Helen**: "Unless taken internally!"	(Page 10)
	Fade to Black-out	

SCENE 2

To open: Interior lighting, afternoon

Cue 2	**Jim** groans	(Page 24)
	Fade to Black-out	

ACT II
SCENE 1

To open: Interior lighting, evening

Cue 3	**Terri** knocks **Bill**'s whisky down his suit	(Page 51)
	Fade to Black-out	

SCENE 2

To open: Interior lighting, evening

Cue 4	As **Helen** ad-libs Chinese dishes	(Page 57)
	Fade to Black-out	

EFFECTS PLOT

ACT I
Scene 1

Cue 1	To open	(Page 1)
	Electronic whoops and whizzes including raspberries can be heard from the study. After a moment, the phone rings	
Cue 2	**Helen** hangs up	(Page 1)
	Computer noise stops	
Cue 3	**Jim** studies the cereal packet and eats	(Page 5)
	Phone rings	

Scene 2

Cue 4	**Edna** is about to resume hoovering	(Page 10)
	Phone rings	
Cue 5	**Jim**: "... had some good times."	(Page 13)
	Phone rings	
Cue 6	**Edna** spits on her duster and cleans vigorously	(Page 13)
	Doorbell rings	
Cue 7	**Jim**: "If you say so, but honestly ... "	(Page 22)
	Phone rings	

ACT II
Scene 1

Cue 8	**Edna** exits	(Page 28)
	Kitchen door shuts	
Cue 9	**Jim** gulps down his drink and pours himself another	(Page 28)
	Doorbell rings	
Cue 10	**Jim**: "... she's got everything under control."	(Page 29)
	Clatter of falling saucepans in the kitchen	
Cue 11	**Bill**: "... prices I'd like to check before dinner."	(Page 30)
	Kitchen door opens	

Cue 12	**Edna** exits to the kitchen *Kitchen door shuts*	(Page 34)
Cue 13	**Edna** turns to go to the kitchen *Doorbell rings*	(Page 48)
Cue 14	**Edna** "... throw around like drunken sailors." *Kitchen door shuts*	(Page 50)

Scene 2

Cue 15	**Terri**: "You bet!" *Phone rings*	(Page 56)
Cue 16	**Helen**: "... Edna's done us a delicious hotpot." *A loud bang is heard from the kitchen*	(Page 57)